MHRA STYLE GUIDE

*A Handbook for
Authors, Editors, and Writers of Theses*

Fourth Edition 2024

Editors
CHLOE PAVER
DEREK CONNON
SIMON F. DAVIES
GERARD LOWE
GRAHAM NELSON
LUCY O'MEARA

Modern Humanities Research Association
2024

Published by the
Modern Humanities Research Association
Salisbury House, Station Road, Cambridge CB1 2LA

ISBN 978-1-83954-248-0
doi:10.59860/msg.b47db8a

MHRA Style Book first published 1971
Second edition 1978
Third edition 1981
Fourth edition 1991
Fifth edition 1996

Revised as the MHRA Style Guide 2002
Second edition 2008
Third edition 2013
Fourth edition 2024

© Modern Humanities Research Association 2024
Licensed under CC BY-NC 4.0.

The Style Guide may be distributed, remixed, adapted, and built upon in any medium or format, provided the usage is noncommercial (not primarily intended for or directed towards commercial advantage or monetary compensation) and provided credit is given to the MHRA.

Contents

INTRODUCTION		5
CHANGES TO MHRA STYLE		7
A QUICK GUIDE TO MHRA STYLE		9
1 PREPARING COPY		
§1.1.	Introduction	14
§1.2.	Preparing the Text	14
§1.3.	Incorporating Illustrations	18
§1.4.	Incorporating Tables	21
2 SPELLING AND PUNCTUATION		
§2.1.	Preferred Spellings	22
§2.2.	Accents	22
§2.3.	Possessives	23
§2.4.	Plurals	24
§2.5.	Commas	25
§2.6.	Hyphens	27
§2.7.	Dashes	28
§2.8.	Parentheses and Brackets	29
§2.9.	Abbreviations	30
§2.10.	Use of Full Stop for Abbreviations	31
§2.11.	Punctuation and Italicization	32
§2.12.	Quotations	32
§2.13.	Short Quotations in Running Text	35
§2.14.	Longer Quotations	36
§2.15.	Quotations from Dramatic Works	37
§2.16.	Footnote and Endnote Numbers	38
3 CAPITALIZATION AND ITALICIZATION		
§3.1.	When to Capitalize	40
§3.2.	Capitalizing Personal Titles and Positions	41
§3.3.	Capitalizing Movements and Periods	42
§3.4.	Capitalizing Titles of Works	42
§3.5.	Compounds	45
§3.6.	Accents on Capitals	46
§3.7.	Italicizing Words	46
§3.8.	Italicizing Titles of Works	47

4 NAMES
- §4.1. Place Names — 50
- §4.2. Academic Institutions — 51
- §4.3. Personal Names — 52
- §4.4. Possessives of Personal Names — 53

5 DATES, NUMBERS, AND QUANTITIES
- §5.1. Dates — 55
- §5.2. Numbers — 56
- §5.3. Roman Numerals — 57
- §5.4. Currency — 57
- §5.5. Weights and Measures — 58

6 DOIs AND URLs
- §6.1. The Difference Between a DOI and a URL — 59
- §6.2. How to Format a DOI — 60
- §6.3. How to Format a URL — 60

7 REFERENCES
- §7.1. Citation in Notes vs Author–Date Citation — 63
- §7.2. Choosing Sources — 64
- §7.3. Citing Books, Chapters, and Literary Works — 64
- §7.4. Citing Journal Articles — 73
- §7.5. Citing Websites and Social Media — 75
- §7.6. Citing Newspaper Articles — 77
- §7.7. Citing Manuscripts — 78
- §7.8. Citing Music, Film, Television, and Software — 79
- §7.9. Citing Works of Art — 81
- §7.10. Citing Theses and Other Unpublished Scholarship — 81
- §7.11. Citing Interviews and Correspondence — 83
- §7.12. Abbreviated References to Works Already Cited — 84
- §7.13. The Author–Date System — 85

8 BIBLIOGRAPHIES AND INDEXES
- §8.1. Inverting Names in Indexes and Bibliographies — 87
- §8.2. Sorting in Alphabetical Order — 89
- §8.3. Bibliography with Citation in Notes — 90
- §8.4. Bibliography with Author–Date Citation — 94
- §8.5. What to Index — 95
- §8.6. Organizing an Index — 96
- §8.7. Index Entries — 97

INDEX — 99

Introduction

A style guide ensures that texts written by different authors, and works by a single author, are presented consistently. Rather than offering advice on rhetorical or argumentative style, a style guide enables writers to follow common practices in the functional elements of writing: spelling, punctuation, and the presentation of numbers, for instance. References to cited sources need to follow a consistent format so that readers and editors can absorb and review the information quickly and follow up references with ease.

As a major academic publisher in the arts and humanities, publishing a wide range of books and journals, the MHRA needs a style guide for the use of its authors and editors. Over the years, the *MHRA Style Guide* has become a key resource for writers and students at all levels.

The *MHRA Style Guide* has always striven to be compact and manageable. It makes no claim to be a comprehensive guide to all issues that might conceivably be encountered by writers in the arts and humanities. Instead, it covers the core issues that are likely to occur in most writing in our fields. These are summarized further in the *Quick Guide* which opens the *Guide*. An author who follows these few guidelines will produce a text that is substantially correct. Where an issue is not covered in the full *Guide*, for instance because the field of study involves unusual text types or ways of encoding information — such as choreography notation or patent applications — specialist advice on style conventions is generally readily available online.

Ten years have passed since the third revised edition of the *MHRA Style Guide* was published. While many aspects of scholarly practice have remained stable, the range of sources used by scholars and the ways that they can be accessed have changed considerably. We have therefore taken the opportunity for a thorough overhaul of the whole *Guide*, including the way in which the information is structured.

In just a few instances we have made alterations to our core style. In each case, this has been done in the interests of usability for both writers and editors. These changes are summarized in *Changes to MHRA Style* below. We hope that these new conventions will establish themselves quickly. There will be a delay while branded referencing software and the 'quick guides to MHRA style' that are provided by university libraries (both of which are beyond the control of the MHRA) catch up with these changes. In the interim, we recommend that university teachers allow old and new forms.

This new edition is for the first time published under the Creative Commons licence CC NC-BY. This allows institutions making use of the *Style Guide* to copy passages and examples freely from our website to their own guidance for students.

Readers who have been using the *Guide* for many years will notice the disappearance of many of the old examples of cited books, journal articles, chapters, and dissertations. Because references were previously retained from one edition to the next, most dated from before 1990. This might not seem to be an issue, given that today's scholars often cite scholarship from the twentieth century. However, the unintended effect of loyalty to existing examples was that whole fields of study and many theoretical approaches not common before 1990 were not represented in the *Guide*. We felt that doctoral and early-career researchers, in particular, would not see their concerns reflected in the examples. The new examples are intended to provide a better reflection of our community's actual range of writing and source materials in the 2020s.

This edition of the *Style Guide* was updated by a team made up of Derek Connon, Simon F. Davies, Gerard Lowe, Graham Nelson, Lucy O'Meara, and Chloe Paver. As today's editors, we are only the current members of an informal committee which began before any of us were born. Though the first *MHRA Style Book*, edited by the Leeds-based scholarly journal printer Stanley Maney and the Shakespeare scholar Robert Smallwood, was not issued until 1971, it codified the work of editors of the *Modern Language Review* who had been meeting since 1905. We acknowledge in particular Glanville Price (chair of the editorial committee in 1991, 1996, 2002) and Brian Richardson (2008, 2013), who saw the last two editions of the *Style Book* and the first three of this modern-format *Style Guide* through press.

Unlike some of the larger US style guides, the *MHRA Style Guide* has no permanent staff. We are unable to enter into correspondence about style or give rulings on instances of style. However, we welcome suggestions for future editions at style@mhra.org.uk.

Changes to MHRA Style

In preparing the fourth edition of the Style Guide (2024), the editors have kept to a bare minimum the changes to core MHRA style since the third edition (2013). The following changes have been made in the interests of simplification and adaptation to digital environments.

1. *Use of 'pp.' for the page extent in references to journal articles:*

   Previously: Susan Sontag, 'Persona', *Sight and Sound*, 36 (1967), 186–212

   Now: Susan Sontag, 'Persona', *Sight and Sound*, 36.4 (1967), pp. 186–212

   A quirk of earlier MHRA style was that it required 'pp.' for chapters in books but omitted it for journal articles. There was no special need for this distinction, which gave extra work to editors and proofreaders. Practice has been simplified by requiring 'pp.' for any run of pages, including journal articles.

2. *Part number even for through-paginated journals:*

   Previously: Claudia Dellacasa, 'Troubled Religiousness in *La cognizione del dolore* by Carlo Emilio Gadda', *MLR*, 115 (2020), 834–51

   Now: Claudia Dellacasa, 'Troubled Religiousness in *La cognizione del dolore* by Carlo Emilio Gadda', *MLR*, 115.4 (2020), pp. 834–51, doi:10.5699/modelangrevi.115.4.0834

   Previously, we required the part number of a journal (e.g. 33.1) only if each part was individually paginated, that is, with Part 2 starting again at page 1. Most articles are now consulted online through journal databases, which divide each year of a journal into its parts. In the new MHRA style, authors give the part number as standard (but without a requirement to also specify the season/month, e.g. Spring 2022).

3. *Requirement for DOIs in journal references:*

   Previously: Roya Biggie, 'The Botany of Colonization in John Fletcher's *The Island Princess*', *Renaissance Drama*, 50 (2022), 159–87

   Now: Roya Biggie, 'The Botany of Colonization in John Fletcher's *The Island Princess*', *Renaissance Drama*, 50.2 (2022), pp. 159–87, doi:10.1086/722938

Nearly all journal articles, even those pre-dating the internet, now have a DOI. Academic writing is increasingly presented online with cross-publication links derived from DOIs, and this practice is likely to become more common. Articles and books which quote DOIs are far better placed to be a part of that emerging scholarly norm than those which do not. The DOI is therefore for the first time required by MHRA style. It is also good practice to supply a DOI where it is available for a book or book chapter.

4. Omission of place of publication unless necessary:

> **Previously:** Susan Harrow, *Zola, the Body Modern: Pressures and Prospects of Representation* (London: Legenda, 2010)
>
> **Now:** Susan Harrow, *Zola, the Body Modern: Pressures and Prospects of Representation* (Legenda, 2010)

For books produced today, place of publication is becoming increasingly arbitrary, especially as publishers merge and agglomerate. The same book may, for instance, have a different place of publication for its printed and ebook versions. In the new MHRA style, place of publication is omitted from references to books, except where it represents useful information for readers, as may be the case with books from the early era of printing, or from printing cultures where publisher names are omitted or uncertain.

A Quick Guide to MHRA Style

This section of the Style Guide summarizes the main features to be noted by authors who are following MHRA style. A full discussion can be found in the chapters and sections indicated. On some points the Guide gives the author choices of style convention: make a consistent choice throughout your text.

Preferred spellings (see §2.1)

Where verbs can end in *-ize* or *-ise*, use *-ize* forms (e.g. *civilize, civilization*), but be aware that some verbs (*revise, exercise*, etc.) always have the *-ise* spelling, and note the British spelling of *analyse*.

Use of full stop for abbreviations (see §2.10)

While the abbreviated form of a full word (e.g. *Prof.*) takes a full stop, a contracted form of a word that ends with the same letter as the full form, including plural *-s*, is not followed by a full stop:

> Prof., Dr, Jr, Mme, Mr, Mrs, St, p., pp., vol., vols

Commas (see §2.5 (c))

In an enumeration of three or more items, the practice in MHRA journals is to insert commas after all but the last item, to give equal weight to each enumerated element: 'The University has departments of French, German, Spanish, and Portuguese within its Faculty of Arts.' The comma after the penultimate item may be omitted in books published by the MHRA, as long as the sense is clear.

Omissions from quotations (see §2.12 (d))

In quotations, points indicating an ellipsis (i.e. the omission of a portion of the text) should be enclosed within square brackets:

> Elizabeth Bowen writes: 'The silence was so intense [...] that no tread could have gained on hers unheard'.

Numbers (see §5.2)

In expressing inclusive numbers falling within the same hundred, the last two figures should be given, including any zero in the penultimate position:

>13–15, 44–47, 100–22, 104–08, 1933–39

Short quotations in running text (see §2.13)

Short quotations (no more than forty words, and no more than two lines of verse) should be enclosed in single quotation marks and run on with the main text. If a verse quotation includes a line division, this should be marked with a spaced upright stroke '|':

> Philip Larkin sees only 'the deep blue air, that shows | Nothing, and is nowhere, and is endless'.

For a quotation within a quotation, double quotation marks should be used.

Unless the quotation forms a complete sentence and is separated from the preceding passage by a punctuation mark, the final full stop should be outside the closing punctuation mark.

Longer quotations (see §2.14)

A long quotation (more than forty words, or more than two lines of verse) should be presented as a paragraph in its own right, with a blank line before and after, and indented.

Long quotations should not be enclosed within quotation marks.

Footnote and endnote numbers (see §2.16)

A note reference number should follow any punctuation except a dash, which it should precede:

> After a comma,[13] not after a dash[14] — but after a full stop.[15]

The text of a note should end with a full stop:

> [13] Like this.

Citation in notes (see §7.1)

If you are writing for publication, your editor will tell you whether to supply your references in the form of notes (footnotes or endnotes) or to use the author–date system. MHRA style supports both. The following sections of the *Quick Guide* show how notes are to be formatted for each of the main types of source and how they are shortened in subsequent references. See below for a short explanation of the alternative author–date notation.

The first time you cite a book in a note (see §7.3 (a)), follow:

> Priyamvada Gopal, *Insurgent Empire: Anticolonial Resistance and British Dissent* (Verso, 2020), p. 63.
>
> *Becoming Visible: Women in European History*, ed. by Renate Bridenthal, Susan Stuard, and Merry E. Wiesner-Hanks, 3rd edn (Houghton Mifflin, 1998).

For a chapter from an edited collection (see §7.3 (b)), follow:

> Ani Kokobobo and Devin McFadden, 'The Queer Nihilist: Queer Time, Social Refusal, and Heteronormativity in *The Precipice*', in *Goncharov in the Twenty-First Century*, ed. by Ingrid Kleespies and Lyudmila Parts (Academic Studies Press, 2021), pp. 132–52 (pp. 146–47), doi:10.2307/j.ctv249sgs4.13.

For a journal article (see §7.4), follow:

> Doriane Zerka, 'Constructing Poetic Identity: Iberia as a Heterotopia in Oswald von Wolkenstein's Songs', *MLR*, 114.2 (2019), pp. 274–93 (p. 279), doi:10.5699/modelangrevi.114.2.0274.

For a play or a longer poem (see §7.3 (c)), follow:

> *The Merchant of Venice*, II. 3. 10.
>
> *Paradise Lost*, IX. 342–50.

For the Bible (see §7.3 (d)), follow:

> Isaiah 22. 17.
>
> II Corinthians 5. 13–15.

For websites and social media (see §7.5), follow:

> Amel Mukhtar, 'How Failure Freed Coco Jones, R&B's Soulful New Star', *British Vogue*, 28 March 2023 <https://www.vogue.co.uk/arts-and-lifestyle/article/coco-jones-interview> [accessed 4 April 2023].
>
> Virago Press (@ViragoBooks), '💙 Some readers have told us they always shed a tear at the ending of Carrie's War', Twitter, 10 April 2023 <https://twitter.com/ViragoBooks/status/1645445347378970624> [accessed 27 April 2023].

For newspaper articles (see §7.6), follow:
> Olivier Ubertalli, 'Entre Antoine Gallimard et Vincent Bolloré, la guerre du livre', *Le Point*, 25 February 2023 <https://www.lepoint.fr/medias/entre-antoine-gallimard-et-vincent-bollore-la-guerre-du-livre-25-02-2023-2509972_260.php> [accessed 3 April 2023].

For audiovisual works and software (see §7.8), follow:
> *The Grapes of Wrath*, dir. by John Ford (USA, 1940).
>
> *Der geteilte Himmel*, dir. by Konrad Wolf (East Germany, 1964).
>
> 'Guy Walks into an Advertising Agency', *Mad Men* (Lionsgate Television, 2007–15), season 3, episode 6 (2009).
>
> Brian Hanrahan, 'East Germany Opens the Gates', *BBC News*, BBC 1, 9 November 1989.

Abbreviated references to works already cited (see §7.12)

In all references to the same source after the first, the shortest intelligible form should be used. The abbreviated reference will normally be the author's name followed by the title (abbreviated where appropriate, for example by dropping any subtitle), the volume number (if applicable), and page reference:
> Zerka, 'Constructing Poetic Identity', p. 281.
>
> Böll, *Werke*, xx, pp. 24–25.

The author–date system (see §7.13)

Author–date is an alternate form of citation in which brief references such as 'Joshua 2020' are used in the text:
> The Romantic age had no settled definition of disability (Joshua 2020).

A fuller description is then given in a bibliography at the end of the work. When writing for journals whose articles do not have bibliographies, this is not possible, but it is a viable option for full-length books, if your editor agrees, or for theses, or student essays. If this system is used, it must be used consistently, either all citations using author–date or none.

References in the text should give in parentheses the surname(s) of the author(s), the publication date of the work, and, where necessary, a page reference, e.g.: '(Joshua 2020: 1–2)'; '(Rye and others 2017)'.

Add initials if you need to distinguish authors with the same surname: '(S. Kemp 2005)', '(A. Kemp 2010)'.

Add letters after the dates if you cite two or more works by the same author from the same year: '(Jones 2017a)', '(Jones 2017b)'.

When the author's name is given in the text, it need not be repeated in the parentheses: 'Smith (2021) argues that...', *not* 'Smith (Smith 2021) argues that...'.

Bibliography with citation in notes (see §8.3)

Bibliography entries, unlike notes, do not end in full stops. In nearly all respects, the material provided in a bibliography matches that provided in notes, as detailed above, in terms of both information and presentation. The main exception to this is the treatment of names. The name of the author or editor of a work is reversed, with the surname preceding the forename, middle name, and/or any initials.

> Gopal, Priyamvada, *Insurgent Empire: Anticolonial Resistance and British Dissent* (Verso, 2020)

Where a work has multiple authors, this applies only to the first author: do not reverse the normal order of names after the first. If a work has more than three authors, list only the first, followed by 'and others'.

> Kokobobo, Ani, and Devin McFadden, 'The Queer Nihilist: Queer Time, Social Refusal, and Heteronormativity in *The Precipice*', in *Goncharov in the Twenty-First Century*, ed. by Ingrid Keespies and Lyudmila Parts (Academic Studies Press, 2021), pp. 132–52, doi:10.2307/j.ctv249sgs4.13

For an edited collection of contributed chapters, the editor's name comes first, inverted as above, followed by 'ed.' or 'eds' as appropriate, placed between brackets:

> Kleespies, Ingrid, and Lyudmila Parts (eds), *Goncharov in the Twenty-First Century* (Academic Studies Press, 2021)

Bibliography with author–date citation (see §8.4)

Bibliographies for books, theses, or essays using author–date citations are almost the same as bibliographies provided with citation in notes, except that the date follows the name of the author(s) or editor(s), with a full stop either side of the date:

> Joshua, Essaka. 2020. *Physical Disability in British Romantic Literature* (Cambridge University Press)
>
> Mukherjee, Paromita. 2021. 'The Non-Human, Haunting, and the Question of "Excess" in Elizabeth Bowen's "The Demon Lover"', *Sanglap*, 8.1, pp. 41–59, doi:10.35684/JLCI.2021.8103

1 • Preparing Copy

> 'Copy' is material sent in to be considered for publication. This chapter deals with the preparation of copy for submission, editing, and subsequent publication in any medium. As such, it will be of more interest to authors than to students, though writers of dissertations might find some of the advice helpful as a supplement to their university's regulations for the presentation of theses.

§1.1. Introduction

When preparing a text for publication, the author should take due account of the 'Guidelines for Contributors' or 'Instructions to Authors' of the journal or series. These will specify the form in which articles or books should be submitted for consideration, and the organization of copy in articles for publication (such as the positioning of abstracts and details of the author's affiliation).

If you are editing a collection of essays, it is your responsibility to ensure that the style is consistent throughout.

Guidelines for contributors will specify what file formats, media, and methods of transmission (e.g. email, file upload) are acceptable. Contact the editor if anything is unclear. The norm is for contributors to submit Microsoft Word documents.

Copy should be carefully checked before initial submission. All quotations should be checked against originals, and not merely against previous drafts of the work. Authors are responsible for the completeness and correctness of references. Ensure that no extraneous comments or queries are embedded in the file.

§1.2. Preparing the Text

(a) Page layout

Do not overdesign your copy since many typographical effects are overridden in typesetting when the publisher's own design is imposed.

It is not advisable to use plug-ins in Microsoft Word (such as automatic citation tools) as they may be incompatible with the software used by your editor or typesetter.

To permit legibility of marginal corrections, use double- or 1.5 times-spacing throughout. Use one size of a simple typeface throughout, including in footnotes or endnotes and extended quotations.

It should be visually clear where a new paragraph begins, either by indenting the text or increased line spacing.

Ensure that page numbering is visible in your document.

(b) Font

Use a serif font such as Times New Roman to avoid confusion of characters such as upper-case 'I' and lower-case 'L', which can look almost identical in sans serif typefaces such as Arial.

(c) Use of bold and capitals

Large capitals (for instance in abbreviations such as BBC or MHRA) should be typed as such. Small capitals are specially designed capitals, the height and visual weight of which approximate to those of lower-case letters. They are normally used for roman volume numbers, postal codes (but not abbreviations for US states), professional and academic qualifications, 'AD', 'BC', 'CE', 'BCE', and 'AH'. They also provide an alternative to italic and bold type in the typographic treatment of subheadings. Where small capitals are required (for instance as volume numbers in references or in postcodes) use the small capitals feature of Microsoft Word, not a reduced font size or full capitals. For further guidance on roman numerals, see §5.3.

Bold should only be used for emphasis in very limited cases, as an alternative to the use of italic, e.g. for highlighting words in the course of lexical analysis. Do not use coloured backgrounds to highlight text.

(d) Headings and subdivisions

Avoid excessive levels of subdivision. Distinguish clearly between headings and subheadings (for instance, by putting headings in bold and subheadings in italics). Capitalize with title case in chapter titles and main headings, and sentence case in sub-headings (see §3.4 for more on title casing). Headings and subheadings should not end with a full stop or colon. For example, a heading and then a subheading:

> German Travel Narratives of the Nineteenth Century
>
> *Humboldt's scientific expeditions to Spanish America*

(e) Spacing

Double spaces should not be used in normal text, and should be eliminated from your copy before submission. Type only a single space between the end of a sentence and the first character of the next, and following major punctuation marks such as colons and semicolons. In quotations from French, do not put a space before a colon, semicolon, exclamation mark, or question mark.

Do not type multiple spaces to indent the first line of a paragraph, or to indent the margin of a quotation: instead, use your word-processor's indentation features.

(f) Non-Latin scripts

Quotations from texts written in non-Latin scripts should generally be given in the original script rather than transliterated. Software is widely available for Cyrillic, Greek, and Han (the extensive set of glyphs used to write Chinese, Japanese, or Korean); editors can advise on scripts written right to left, such as Arabic or Hebrew, where computing support is less certain and practical considerations may need to override stylistic ideals. The same applies to left-to-right but unusual scripts, such as Egyptian hieroglyphs.

While quoted material should in general not be transliterated, names of people or places outside of quotations should be. Thus, 'Gogol'' took up residence in Moscow', not 'Гоголь took up residence in Москва'. See §4.1 (b) for place names which have a standard English form; these should be used in preference to a transliteration, where that would produce a different spelling.

Similarly, words or phrases being discussed as such, rather than as quotations, are normally transliterated: thus, 'Ivan's division of Russia into *oprichnina* and *zemshchina* led to a period now known as the *Smutnoe vremia*'. Single words and short phrases in languages other than English are italicized. However, words that have passed into regular English usage, such as glasnost or samizdat, need not be italicized. (See §3.7 (b).)

Titles of books, articles, or poems originally written in Slavonic languages (such as Russian, but also Belarusian, Ukrainian, and Bulgarian) should always be transliterated where they appear in discussions or bibliographies, and this must be done consistently, following the same system used for names: see below. In other language areas, conventions differ, and authors should make a pragmatic decision. In cases where an untransliterated title does appear, a translation may be needed to assist the reader. For example, the following bibliography entry might appear in a book aimed at art historians who are not necessarily specialists in Japanese:

> Yanaihara, Isaku, 完本 ジャコメッティ手帖 [The Complete Giacometti Handbook], 2 vols (Misuzu Shobo, 2010)

Where possible, use an existing standard scheme for transliteration. For many languages, a standard Romanization table is provided by ALA-LC, a collaboration of the American Library Association and the Library of Congress. These tables are easy to find online and simple to apply: however, ALA-LC does sometimes need to be adapted or extended for scholarly use. For example, in Arabic studies scholars often follow IJMES style.

For Slavonic languages, MHRA style is to use ALA-LC but without diacritics (i.e. without breve, macron, or dot accents). For instance:

> Dostoevskii, Chaikovskii, Tolstoi, Evtushenko, Gogol′, Gor′kii, Il′ia

For the soft sign ь use the prime symbol ′ (Unicode U+2032) and *not* an apostrophe '. For example, 'Gogol′'s infamous lectures of 1834'. Similarly, the less common hard sign ъ should use the double prime ″ (Unicode U+2033) and *not* a double-quotation mark ".

When writing outside the context of Slavonic studies, for example in a comparative literature article, authors may instead choose to follow common English forms, provided they do so consistently. Thus the following are acceptable:

> Dostoevsky, Tchaikovsky, Tolstoy, Yevtushenko

(g) The International Phonetic Alphabet

A special case among non-Latin scripts is the International Phonetic Alphabet (IPA), used in linguistics to represent the range of sounds which form human speech. It is normal practice to enclose the use of IPA within slashes or square brackets: slashes are used for phonemic notation (denoting the abstract or mental representation of the sound unit) whereas square brackets are used for phonetic notation (representing the actual pronunciation of the sounds). For example, Marcel Proust's surname has the phonemic representation /pʁust/, but is pronounced [pʁ̥ust], with progressive devoicing of the voiced uvular fricative, /ʁ/, marked by an IPA diacritic. Graphemes, or letters — such as ⟨b⟩ or ⟨a⟩ — appear in angled brackets.

Your editor can advise on software for accessing the full range of IPA characters. All of the material inside the slashes or square brackets should use the same IPA font. The International Phonetic Association recommends that IPA material should never be italicized.

(h) Cross-references

Since they cannot be finalized until the text is typeset, cross-references within an article or book should be typed as triple zeros:

> See above [or below], p. 000, n. 000.

Internal cross-referencing, i.e. cross-references to pages within your own document, should be avoided as far as possible, for instance by giving references to chapters, sections, or notes: 'See Chapter 3', 'See Section 4.3', 'See Chapter 4, n. 000', 'See n. 000'. Use 'above' and 'below', not 'supra' and 'infra'. Where you need to repeat a reference to the same source, follow the guidelines in §7.12 below rather than cross-referencing to another note. Where internal cross-referencing to a page is unavoidable, cross-references should be carefully checked and marked on the proofs. Do not use Microsoft Word plugins or extension software which embeds citations or URLs: type or copy these in normal text.

§1.3. Incorporating Illustrations

(a) Numbering and placement

Discuss the inclusion of any illustrative material with your editor prior to submission. For all illustrations that are in copyright, you must obtain, from all interested rights-owners, written permission to reproduce in all publication formats (print or electronic), including confirmation of the credit to be printed acknowledging permission to reproduce. Permission documents should be supplied with the illustrations.

All illustrations should be supplied electronically. The appropriate resolution, file format, and means of submission should be discussed with the editor. All illustrations should be supplied as separate files, not embedded within the text. Give each illustration a clear filename that includes the figure number.

Illustrations, usually referred to as 'figures', should be numbered. For an article, number from 1 upwards; if a single figure combines two or more images to be displayed side by side (for example, for comparison or to show a succession of frames from a film), individual images should be identified as (a), (b), (c), and so on. Within a chapter for a monograph or edited book, number figures within each chapter: thus Chapter 3 would have Figures 3.1, 3.2, and so on. When referring to an image within your own text, use a figure number, as an illustration may not immediately follow the relevant text, for reasons of layout. For example: 'Courbet's painting (Fig. 1.1), begun at Étretat in the summer of 1869, caused a small sensation on its exhibition the following year.'

To indicate where the image should be placed, insert a standalone paragraph at the point in the text where you want the image to appear, consisting of the phrase 'Figure [...]', followed by the caption.

(b) Captions

Each figure should have a caption, which will usually be printed beneath it. A caption should begin 'FIG.' (note the small capitals), then give the figure number, then a full stop. The caption should identify the image briefly but self-sufficiently, that is, so that the caption alone would be enough to tell the reader what this is a picture of. Visual material is so varied that no single set of rules will cover every eventuality, but the following guidance may be helpful.

For works of art, captions usually follow the form:

> Artist, *Title* (year), materials, dimensions in cm. Gallery or museum (or 'private collection'). © Copyright acknowledgement if needed.

Artist names should usually be more than surnames (so, 'Paul Cézanne', not 'Cézanne') but no longer than needed for clear identification (so, 'Henri Rousseau', not 'Henri Julien Félix Rousseau, known as Le Douanier'). If a commonly used English title exists for an artwork (e.g. *The Birth of Venus*) it should generally be used. Whether or not materials and dimensions are included will depend on the conventions of the particular field of visual study; authors should aim to be consistent across their figures. If giving dimensions, note the use of a multiplication sign, not a lower case 'x', and the spaces around it.

Captions differ from notes and bibliography entries in that they may require acknowledgement of copyright; information about rights-owners is omitted from any note or bibliography entry that refers to the same image or to the film or broadcast from which it is taken. If the rights-owners have requested an exact form of words for the copyright acknowledgment, this wording must be used. See §7.9.

Analysis of the image should be placed in the main text, not a caption. If any comment follows, drawing the reader's attention to something, it should come at the end of the caption and be kept brief.

For example:

> FIG. 1.1. Gustave Courbet, *La Mer orageuse (La Vague)* (Salon of 1870), oil on canvas, 116 × 160 cm. Musée d'Orsay, Paris. Guy de Maupassant later described seeing Courbet pressing his face to the window to look out at this storm, and slapping white paint on a blank canvas with a kitchen knife.
>
> FIG. 1.2. Alberto Giacometti, untitled drawing (1964), lithographic pencil on transfer paper, 42 × 32.6 cm. Published in *Paris sans fin* (1969), plate 38. © Succession Alberto Giacometti / Sabam, Belgium, 2022. Photo credit: Fondation Giacometti, Paris.
>
> FIG. 1.3. Franz Ludwig Catel, *Gulf of Naples* (1831) (detail). Germanisches Nationalmuseum, Nuremberg; on loan from the Kunstsammlungen der Stadt Nürnberg. © J. Musolf.

Where captions are to film or television stills, there is often no single artist, though it is usual to credit a director. The studio or production company (as the rights-owner), and date, should be given in brackets. If positions within a film are needed, they should be given in hours-minutes-seconds format, i.e. HH:MM:SS, or MM:SS for shorter formats. For example:

> FIG. 2.1. *Jaurès* (La Huit Production, 2012), dir. Vincent Dieutre. © La Huit/Cinaps TV.
>
> FIG. 2.2. Solomon Perel appears as himself in the final sequence of *Hitlerjunge Salomon* (Central Cinema Company Film, 1992), dir. Agnieszka Holland (01:45:27).

Where captions are to printed material, such as book frontispieces, newspaper pages, or cartoons from magazines, give the publication and date. For daily newspapers, the day, month, and year should be given; for magazines numbering their issues, the number and year. For example:

> FIG. 3.1. Cartoon in *O António Maria* (21 February 1884), depicting Guiomar Torresão and the Marquês de Valada.
>
> FIG. 3.2. 'La crainte d'être apperçue arrêtoit jusqu'à ma respiration', engraved by L. M. Halbou after Le Barbier *l'aîné*, in Françoise de Graffigny, *Lettres d'une Péruvienne* [...] *traduites du Français en Italien par M. Deodati* (Mignaret, 1797). Private collection.

For photographs other than art photographs or photographs of artworks, the caption will normally identify what is in the image, give the name of the photographer (if known and relevant), the year in which it was taken, and the source of the image. A copyright statement should be made where required, using any wording requested by the rights-owner. Be particularly careful to date any scene that shows a historical artefact, streetscape, or landscape that has changed since the image was taken. If it is not possible to date an image or if only an approximate dating is possible, that information may still be of use to the reader.

> Fig. 4.1. Information boards at the Nazi Party Rally Grounds, 2003. These information boards were replaced in 2006. Photograph taken by the author.

> Fig. 4.2. Dürer House, Nuremberg, as it was in 1930. Stadtarchiv Nürnberg. A 38 Nr. D-18-1.

Since all the source information is given in the caption, it is not necessary also to supply this information in a footnote or endnote.

§1.4. Incorporating Tables

Tables should be prepared using Microsoft Word's standard table function. It is not normally necessary to supply them as separate files; insert the table in roughly the position you would like it to appear. In your discussion, refer to tables as 'Table 1.1', 'Table 1.2', etc. Number tables consecutively within each chapter. Supply a title for each table, in the form:

> Table 4.1. Narrating instances model for the *Comedy*, derived from analysis of *Inferno* I and *Paradiso* XXXIII.

A table title ends with a full stop. Note that, for reasons of page layout, it may not be possible for the table to be printed in the exact position that you have requested.

Bear in mind, when producing your table, that printed books and journals typically provide less room between the margins for text than your software does. For example, Microsoft Word offers the author a full A4 page on which a very complicated table can be made, but that may be two or three times larger than can fit on a book or journal page.

2 • Spelling and Punctuation

This chapter covers the most common issues of spelling and punctuation. Since MHRA authors regularly work on the literatures and cultures of Europe and the European diaspora, we offer particular guidance on the use of accents (diacritics) and the spellings of words borrowed or imported from other languages. These words sometimes also need to be italicized or capitalized; that aspect is dealt with in Chapter 3. For the many examples of spellings and hyphenation that are beyond the scope of this short guide, a good dictionary will offer an acceptable solution. The 'New Oxford Dictionary for Writers and Editors', for instance, can resolve many common queries. For scholarly work, rules also need to be set for the punctuation used in quotations and for punctuation in relation to footnotes and endnotes. Since we deal with quotations at length in this chapter, we have included related advice on how to lay them out.

§2.1. Preferred Spellings

Where verbs can end in *-ize* or *-ise*, use *-ize* forms (e.g. *civilize, civilization*), but be aware that some verbs must have the *-ise* spelling, e.g.:

> advertise, advise, apprise, chastise, comprise, compromise, demise, despise, devise, enterprise, excise, exercise, franchise, improvise, incise, revise, supervise, surmise, surprise, televise

The British spelling of *analyse* and its derivatives has *s* and not *z*. Similarly, *catalyse* and *paralyse*.

Some book-length projects otherwise following MHRA style prefer *-ise* to *-ize*. Check with your editor before making this choice, and ensure that it is followed consistently in every chapter.

The forms *disk, program* are used even in British spelling in computing contexts; otherwise, use *disc, programme*.

§2.2. Accents

There is great inconsistency between dictionaries, and sometimes within the same dictionary, as to the use of accents (or other diacritics) in words borrowed from other languages. Two cases, however, are clear:

(a) When a word or, more often, an expression is still felt to be a borrowing from another language (and an objective decision is not always possible), all accents should be retained, e.g.:

> aide-mémoire, à la mode, *ancien régime*, belle époque, bête noire, cause célèbre, déjà vu, doppelgänger, *éminence grise, fin de siècle,* lycée, maître d'hôtel, papier mâché, *pièce de résistance, raison d'être,* Señor, *succès de scandale,* tête-à-tête

Whether a word with accents is capitalized or italicized depends on different sets of conventions: see §3.1 and subsequent sections (capitalization) and §3.7 and subsequent sections (italicization).

(b) Words ending in -*é* retain their accent:

> blasé, café, cliché, communiqué, exposé, fiancé *and* fiancée

In such words, any other accents are also retained, e.g.:

> émigré, pâté, protégé, résumé

(c) We recommend that, except as provided for in (b) above, accents should be dropped in the case of words that have passed into regular English usage, e.g.:

> chateau, debacle, debris, decor, denouement, detente, echelon, elite, fete, hotel, matinee, naive, precis, premiere, regime, role, seance

For the use of accents on capitals, see §3.6.

§2.3. Possessives

The possessive of nouns and indefinite pronouns is regularly formed by the addition of -*s* preceded by the apostrophe:

> the court's decision
> a month's worth of rain
> the witness's testimony
> Smith's elixir
> no one's fault
> the children's day out

The possessive forms of personal pronouns *hers, its, theirs, yours* do not have an apostrophe.

In plural nouns ending in -*s* the possessive is represented by the apostrophe alone:

> the courts' decisions

months' worth of planning
the witnesses' testimonies
MPs' assistants

For possessives of personal names, see §4.4.

§2.4. Plurals

Some nouns borrowed from foreign languages have only the regular English plural, e.g.:

(*Greek*) metropolis, metropolises

(*Latin*) campus, campuses; census, censuses; album, albums; museum, museums; premium, premiums

(*Italian*) canto, cantos; soprano, sopranos; sonata, sonatas

(*German*) Junker, Junkers

Some nouns, especially ones adopted from Greek and Latin, have only the foreign plural ending, e.g.:

(*Greek*) analysis, analyses; axis, axes; basis, bases; crisis, crises; diagnosis, diagnoses; oasis, oases; thesis, theses (and similarly with hypothesis, parenthesis, synthesis); criterion, criteria; phenomenon, phenomena

(*Latin*) alumnus, alumni; stimulus, stimuli; addendum, addenda; datum, data; desideratum, desiderata; erratum, errata; codex, codices

(*German*) lied, lieder

Other borrowed nouns may have either the English or the foreign plural. In general, the foreign plural is less common and more formal, or it may have a more specialized sense, as in these words of Greek or Latin origin:

formula (formulas in everyday usage, formulae in specialized contexts)

thesaurus (thesauruses, thesauri)

medium (mediums in spiritualism, media for (plural) means of communication)

memorandum (memorandums, memoranda)

referendum (referendums, referenda)

ultimatum (ultimatums, ultimata)

corpus (corpuses, corpora)

appendix (appendixes for parts of the body, appendixes or appendices for additional parts of a publication) index (indexes for alphabetical lists of references, indices in mathematics)

Some adopted French words may retain the original plural -*x*, but -*s* has become more common. For example, *adieu* is normally pluralized *adieus* rather than *adieux*.

In academic argument, authors should consider their reader's likely language knowledge before using loan words in the plural form, since not all plural endings are readily recognizable as such. A translation or gloss may be preferable. The following statement, in which the first loan word is plural and the second singular, is acceptable for an article targeted at German specialists:

> During the 1990s, the Länder clashed repeatedly with the Bund on this issue.

For a wider readership it would be preferable to write:

> During the 1990s, the German federal states (the Länder) clashed repeatedly with central government on this issue.

See also §5.4 on the plurals of foreign currencies.

No apostrophe should be used before the plural ending of abbreviations, names, numbers, letters, and words not normally used as nouns, e.g.:

> MPs, POWs, PhDs
> the Henrys, the two Germanys
> the 1960s, the twenties, ones and twos
> *a*s and *e*s, the three Rs
> haves and have nots

§2.5. Commas

Commas are used singly or in pairs to group or separate words in a sentence. Particular note should be taken of the following usages:

(a) To delimit phrases

Commas should be used in pairs to delimit parenthetical or interpolated phrases, and nouns in apposition:

> My father, not to mention the rest of my family, felt the loss deeply.
> This book, written in 1505, would change the world.
> Dante, the Florentine poet, was born around 1265.

No commas are needed if a defining phrase precedes the noun:
> The Florentine poet Dante was born around 1265.
> The film director Maren Ade was nominated for an Oscar in 2016.

In such a case, the person's name would only be enclosed in commas if they are the sole example of the defining phrase or if they had been mentioned obliquely in a previous sentence and were now being introduced by name. For example:
> The then Prime Minister, Clement Attlee, faced a series of foreign-policy challenges.
> The prize jury consists of two screenwriters, a film director, and a cinematographer. The film director, Maren Ade, was nominated for an Oscar in 2016.

(b) To show that a relative clause applies to a category

Commas are used where a relative clause applies to the whole of the category named:
> Those with a university degree, who have experience of higher education, see qualifications in a different light.
> The family had two cats, which slept indoors, and a rabbit.

No commas are used where the relative clause applies only to some of the category:
> Those with a university degree who have studied medicine see research in a different light.
> The family had two cats which slept indoors and one which went out at night.

(c) To divide items in a list

In an enumeration of three or more items, the practice in MHRA journals is to insert commas after all but the last item, to give equal weight to each enumerated element:
> The University has departments of French, German, Spanish, and Portuguese within its Faculty of Arts.

The conjunctions *and* and *or* without a preceding comma are understood as linking the parts of a single enumerated element:
> The University has departments of French, German, Spanish and Portuguese, Czech and Polish, and Dutch.
> The study could include comedians such as Laurel and Hardy, Abbott and Costello, or Victoria Wood.

By the same principle a comma should be used before a phrase such as 'and so on' or 'etc.' at the end of an enumeration.

(d) Omission where unnecessary

Commas should not be used if their omission leaves the meaning of the sentence unaffected. The mere fact that a sentence has a lengthy subject does not justify the use of a comma between the subject and verb. Accordingly a sentence such as the following requires no comma after 'handbook':

> The team of editors which was responsible for the latest edition of the handbook has made a significant number of changes.

§2.6. Hyphens

Hyphens occasionally occur within the body of a word, particularly with *re-* followed by *e* (e.g. *re-echo, re-enter*), but they normally indicate that two or more words are to be read as a single word with only one main stress. The examples given on the left below show forms that are attributive and have a single main stress and are therefore hyphenated, while predicative and other forms having two main stresses (shown on the right) are not hyphenated:

attributive	predicative
a well-known fact	the facts are well known
a tenth-century manuscript	in the tenth century

Where there is no possibility of ambiguity, only one hyphen need be used in a multiple-word attributive (but see below on *mid-*): for example, *a late eighteenth-century novelist* and *post-Second World War difficulties* are to be preferred to *a late-eighteenth-century novelist* and *post-Second-World-War difficulties*.

In phrases where two or more parallel hyphenated terms are combined, the first hyphen is followed by a space: e.g. *pre- and post-war governments, pro- and anti-abortion movements, eighteenth- and nineteenth-century literature*.

Adverbs ending in *-ly* and other polysyllabic adverbs are not hyphenated to a following adjective or participle:

> a highly contentious argument
> a recently published novel
> a handsomely bound volume
> a frequently occurring mistake

> a hitherto unrecognized custom
> ever increasing quantities

Some monosyllabic adverbs (in particular *ill* but not *well* — see above) followed by a participle have only one main stress and are therefore hyphenated even when used predicatively:

> He is very ill-tempered.
> Such a course of action would be ill-advised.
> These prejudices are deep-seated.

The prefix *mid-* always requires a hyphen (except where it forms part of a single word, as in *midnight*):

> The boat sank in mid-Atlantic.
> a mid-June midnight flight
> a mid-sixteenth-century chair
> until the mid-nineteenth century

The presence or absence of a hyphen is often significant:

with	without
two-year-old dogs	two year-old dogs
a deep-blue lake	a deep blue lake
a pro-vice-chancellor	a pro-vice chancellor
to re-cover	to recover

There is considerable variation in the use of hyphens. Use a dictionary such as the *New Oxford Dictionary for Writers and Editors* and be consistent. Some words that used to be hyphenated are now single unhyphenated words:

> webpage, bestseller, overrun, overleaf, subtitle

Some authors may prefer to use either a hyphenated or unhyphenated version of a core term in their field, such as *post-colonial* or *postcolonial*. In such cases, the MHRA will normally accept the author's preference, but usage should be consistent throughout.

§2.7. Dashes

In addition to hyphens, scholarly writing uses both a short and a long dash or 'rule'.

The short dash ('en-rule') is used to indicate a span or a differentiation and may be considered a substitute for 'and' or 'to':

> the England–France match
> the 1939–45 war
> 2 January–13 February
> pp. 81–101

(For further guidance on date ranges, see §5.1.) However, compound adjectives take a hyphen and not a dash; thus 'Sino-Soviet relations' but 'the Molotov–Ribbentrop Pact'.

Long dashes ('em-rules'), with a space on either side, are normally found in pairs to enclose parenthetical statements, or singly to denote a break in the sentence:

> Some people — an ever increasing number — deplore this.
> Family and fortune, health and happiness — all were gone.

Long dashes should not be over-used; commas, colons, or parentheses are often more appropriate. When more than one set of long dashes are used in a single sentence, it is unlikely to read clearly. Punctuation marks such as commas should not normally be used before or after a dash.

A very long dash '——', known as a 2-em rule, is used to indicate 'ditto' in bibliographies and similar lists:

> Marlowe, Christopher, *Edward II*
> —— *The Jew of Malta*

§2.8. Parentheses and Brackets

The forms of brackets most commonly used in scholarly writing are: square brackets [thus], round brackets or 'parentheses' (thus), angle brackets ⟨thus⟩, and braces {thus}.

Parentheses, i.e. round brackets, are used for parenthetical statements and references within a text. When a passage within parentheses falls at the end of a sentence of which it is only a part, the final full stop is placed outside the closing parenthesis:

> This was well reviewed at the time (for instance in *TLS*, 9 July 1971, p. 817).

Since a pair of brackets serves a similar function to a pair of commas in creating a parenthesis, a comma is never placed before an opening bracket.

When a complete sentence is within parentheses, the final full stop should be inside the closing parenthesis. Parentheses may be used within parentheses:

(His presidential address (1967) made this point clearly.)

Do not alternate round and square brackets in such a case. Square brackets should be used only for the enclosure of phrases or words which have been added to the original text or for editorial and similar comments:

He adds that 'the lady [Mrs Jervis] had suffered great misfortunes'.
I do not think they should have [*two words illegible*].
He swore to tell the truth, the old [*sic*] truth, and nothing but the truth.

For translations following quotations in another language use either square brackets or round brackets consistently, in accordance with the style conventions of the journal or book series you are writing for.

For the use of square brackets around ellipses, see §2.12 (d). For the use of square brackets around access dates for websites, and angle brackets around URLs, see §6.3.

§2.9. Abbreviations

Since abbreviations increase the possibility of confusion and misunderstanding, they should be used only where there is no possibility of ambiguity. When writing for a particular publication, use only those abbreviations which are likely to be familiar to its readers. Never begin a sentence with an abbreviation, and avoid abbreviations as far as possible in passages of continuous prose. For example:

The author's comments on page 47, line 20, of his manuscript seem particularly apt.

Here the words 'page' and 'line', normally abbreviated in references, are given in full to prevent a disruptive effect in reading.

If your particular topic or argument requires extensive use of abbreviations, other than common ones such as 'p.' and 'l.', list them at the beginning of your book or in an early note to your article or chapter.

To avoid frequent repetition of a title, especially a long one, abbreviation will from time to time be needed. In the body text, this should normally take the form of a short title, e.g. *A la recherche* for *A la recherche du temps perdu*, *Two Gentlemen* for *Two Gentlemen of Verona*. In notes, and in parenthetical textual references in the main body of a book or article, abbreviations are more often appropriate, e.g. *ALR* or *TGV*. Follow conventional abbreviations where these exist, e.g. OED for *Oxford English Dictionary*, or PMC for *Poema de mio Cid*.

§2.10. Use of Full Stop for Abbreviations

A contracted form of a word that ends with the same letter as the full form, including plural -*s*, is not followed by a full stop:

> Dr, Jr, Mme, Mr, Mrs, St, vols

But note the exception 'no.' from Italian 'numero', plural 'nos.'. Other abbreviations take a full stop and are followed by a space unless they fall at the end of a sentence:

> M. Dupont (Monsieur), Prof. J. Jones, ibid., l. 6, ll. 22–28, p. 6, pp. 106–09, vol. XIX

Note in particular abbreviations relating to editing:

> ed. by *but* edn (*for* edition), eds

In lower-case abbreviations for expressions consisting of more than one word, there is a full stop after each initial:

> a.m. (*ante meridiem*), e.g. (*exempli gratia*), i.e. (*id est*), n.p. (no place [of publication]), n.d. (no date [of publication])

Full stops are omitted in capitalized abbreviations or acronyms for:

(a) standard works of reference (italicized), journals (italicized), or series (not italicized):

> *DNB*, *OED*, *ABELL*, *MLR*, *PMLA*, *TLS*, BAR, PMHRS, PRF, TBL

(b) countries, institutions, societies, and organizations (none of them italicized):

> UK, USA, BL, BM, UNAM, CNRS, ANTS, MHRA, MLA, UNESCO

(c) the standard abbreviations in bibliographical references for 'manuscript', 'manuscripts':

> MS, MSS

(d) the two-letter postal abbreviations for American states, e.g.:

> CA (California), IL (Illinois), MA (Massachusetts), NY (New York)

These have largely replaced older abbreviations such as 'Calif.'. Lists of the abbreviations are widely available online.

Note the correct form of the name of Washington, DC (comma, no stops).

(e) names of academic degrees, e.g.:

>MA, MPhil, PhD

§2.11. Punctuation and Italicization

There are italic forms of most marks of punctuation. The type style (roman or italics) of the main part of any sentence will govern the style of the punctuation marks within or concluding it. If the main part of a sentence is in roman but an italic word within it immediately precedes a mark of punctuation, that mark will normally be in roman.

However, if the punctuation mark occurs within a phrase or title which is entirely in italics, or if the punctuation mark belongs to the phrase in italics rather than to the sentence as a whole, the punctuation mark will be in italics:

> Where is a storm more brilliantly portrayed than in Conrad's *Typhoon*?
>
> In *Edmund Ironside; or, War Hath Made All Friends*, a play that survives in manuscript, we see this technique in operation.
>
> Kingsley followed this with *Westward Ho!*, perhaps his best-known novel.
>
> Who wrote *Who's Afraid of Virginia Woolf?*?

Do not substitute roman for italics in titles within italicized titles; in such cases, single quotation marks should be used even if they do not figure in the original, e.g. *The Music and the Myth: Wagner's 'Ring' and its Symbols* not *The Music and the Myth: Wagner's* Ring *and its Symbols*.

For more general advice on italicization, see §3.7 and §3.8.

§2.12. Quotations

Quotation marks should normally be reserved for indicating direct quotations, definitions of words, or for otherwise highlighting a word or phrase. Avoid the practice of using quotation marks to indicate a loose, slang, or imprecise word or phrase.

Translations of quoted material should normally follow the original in the main text, rather than being placed in the notes. They should be enclosed in quotation marks and set in either square or round brackets consistently. If round brackets are used, then for example:

> Curtius's formulation of the 'locus amoenus' ('pleasant place') is exemplified by Dante in *Purgatorio* XXVIII: 'qui primavera sempre e ogne frutto' ('here evermore was spring, and every fruit').

And if the square-brackets convention is followed:

> Curtius's formulation of the 'locus amoenus' ['pleasant place'] is exemplified by Dante in *Purgatorio* XXVIII: 'qui primavera sempre e ogne frutto' ['here evermore was spring, and every fruit'].

(a) Short vs long quotations

Prose quotations of no more than forty words in a single paragraph or verse quotations of no more than two lines are considered short quotations, and are to be treated as in §2.13 below. All other quotations should be treated as long quotations, as in §2.14 below. If, however, several short quotations come close together and are compared or contrasted or otherwise set out as examples, it may be appropriate to treat them together as a long quotation.

(b) Spelling in quotations

In quoted passages follow the original for spelling, capitalization, and italics. Note, however, that in quotations from early printed books the forms of the letters *i* and *j*, *u* and *v*, the long *s* (ſ or ſ), the ampersand (&), the Tironian sign (⁊), the tilde, superior (superscript) letters in contractions, and other abbreviations may be normalized to modern usage.

(c) Punctuation in quotations

In quoted passages from English, follow the punctuation of the original.

Quotations in languages other than English are treated in the same way, but unless there are special reasons to the contrary, the forms of quotation marks in foreign languages («...», „...", etc.) should be normalized to English usage. In long quotations, a long dash (em-dash) may be used to introduce dialogue in prose from languages such as French and Russian. Spacing before and after punctuation should respect English-language norms.

(d) Omissions from quotations

Omissions within prose quotations should be marked by an ellipsis (three points within square brackets):

> Her enquiries [...] were not very favourably answered.

This makes it possible to distinguish between points indicating an ellipsis and points that occur in the original, as they do in the following quotations:

> Will you never have done ... revolving it all?
>
> Well, he's completely mad, of course. They all are...

It is not normally necessary to use an ellipsis at the beginning or end of a quotation; almost all quotations will be taken from a larger context and there is usually no need to indicate this obvious fact unless the sense of the passage quoted is manifestly incomplete. Square brackets normally remain in roman type even if the text being quoted is in italics.

Omitted lines of verse should be marked by an ellipsis on a separate line:

> I am not covetous for gold,
> [...]
> But if it be a sin to covet honour
> I am the most offending soul alive.

The original punctuation is retained when it is possible to do so:

> When, in the course of human events, it becomes necessary for one people to dissolve the political bands which have connected them with another [...], a decent respect to the opinions of mankind requires that they should declare the causes which impel them to the separation.
>
> Outside the hut I stood bemused. [...] It was still morning and the smoke from the cookhouse rose straight to the leaden sky.

It may be necessary to add punctuation or change from upper case to lower case (or vice versa) to ensure that a sentence with ellipses remains correctly punctuated. When the beginning of a sentence is omitted, the first word following the ellipsis can be capitalized even if it does not have a capital in the original:

> For the rest of the evening, von Igelfeld considered his response. [...] He could just ignore the article altogether.

(In the original, the passage abbreviated ends 'And finally, he could just ignore the article altogether'.)

Except in detailed textual scholarship, there is no need to use square brackets to indicate a change of capitalization. For instance,

> The narrator describes 'fog creeping into the cabooses of collier-brigs'.

is normally preferable to

> The narrator describes '[f]og creeping into the cabooses of collier-brigs'.

§2.13. Short Quotations in Running Text

Short quotations should be enclosed in single quotation marks and run on with the main text. If a verse quotation includes a line division, this should be marked with a spaced upright stroke ' | '.

> Balzac's famous observation 'Je suis en train de devenir un génie' has generated much sceptical comment.
> 'I had seen birth and death | But had thought they were different', muses Eliot's Wise Man.

For a quotation within a quotation, double quotation marks should be used:

> Mrs Grose replies that 'Master Miles only said "We must do nothing but what she likes!"'.

If a short quotation is used at the end of a sentence, the final full stop should be outside the closing quotation mark:

> Do not be afraid of what Stevenson calls 'a little judicious levity'.

This rule applies even when a quotation ends with a full stop in the original, and when a quotation forms a complete sentence in the original but, as quoted, is integrated within a sentence of introduction or comment without intervening punctuation:

> We learn at once that 'Miss Brooke had that kind of beauty which seems to be thrown into relief by poor dress'.

For quotations which are either interrogatory or exclamatory, punctuation marks should appear both before and after the closing quotation mark:

> The pause is followed by Richard's demanding 'will no man say "Amen"?'.
> Why does Shakespeare give Malcolm the banal question 'Oh, by whom?'?

The final full stop should precede the closing quotation mark only when the quotation forms a complete sentence and is separated from the preceding passage by a punctuation mark. Such a quotation may be interrupted:

> Wilde said, 'He found in stones the sermons he had already hidden there.'
> Soames added: 'Well, I hope you both enjoy yourselves.'
> Hardy's *Satires of Circumstance* was not well received. 'The gloom', wrote Lytton Strachey in his review of it, 'is not even relieved by a little elegance of diction.'

In this last example, the comma after 'gloom' follows the quotation mark as there is no comma in the original. Contrast:

'It is a far, far better thing that I do,' Carton asserts, 'than I have ever done.'

Here the original has a comma after 'I do'. But when the quotation ends in a question mark or an exclamation mark, it is not followed by a comma:

'What think you of books?' said he.

When a short quotation is followed by a reference in parentheses, the final punctuation should follow the closing parenthesis:

He assumes the effect to be 'quite deliberate' (p. 29).

There is no reason to doubt the effect of this 'secret humiliation' (Book VI, Chapter 52).

§2.14. Longer Quotations

A long quotation should be presented as a paragraph in its own right, with a blank line before and after, and left-indented. A long quotation should never be used in the middle of a sentence of the main text: it is unreasonable to expect the reader to carry the sense of a sentence across a quotation several lines in length. Long quotations are not normally placed in footnotes or endnotes.

Long quotations should not be enclosed within quotation marks. A quotation occurring within such a long quotation should be in single quotation marks; if a further quotation occurs within that, double quotation marks should be used. Foreign forms of quotation marks (see §2.12 (c)) should not be preserved unless there are special reasons for doing so.

The first line of a long prose quotation should be indented only if the quotation consists of more than one paragraph and the first line starts a paragraph in the original. Verse quotations should follow the layout and indentation of the original.

Long quotations should normally end with a full stop; even though the original may use other punctuation, there is no need (except for a question mark or exclamation mark) to preserve this at the end of a quotation. There is no need to put square brackets around a full stop when it is not in the original.

Avoid interpolations that introduce square brackets into the opening lines of long quotations, e.g.:

This play [writes Samuel Johnson, referring to *Cymbeline*] has many just sentiments, some natural dialogues, and some pleasing scenes, but they are obtained at the expense of much incongruity.

The need for any such formulation can be eliminated by some such rephrasing as the following:

> Referring to *Cymbeline*, Samuel Johnson writes:
>> This play has many just sentiments, some natural dialogues, and some pleasing scenes.

A reference in parentheses after a long quotation should always be placed outside the closing full stop, and without a full stop of its own (see examples in §2.15).

When any substantial amount of text is being quoted from a text still in copyright — particularly if whole poems or song lyrics are quoted — authors should be aware that this may not fall under the copyright exceptions which allow reasonable use of quotation for scholarly purposes. Legal permission may need to be sought and this is generally the author's responsibility. Editors can advise on this.

§2.15. Quotations from Dramatic Works

Where a quotation from a play is longer than about forty words, or two lines of verse, it should be treated as a long quotation (see §2.14). While the spelling and punctuation within the text should be preserved, general rules may be applied to the treatment of speakers' names and stage directions.

Where a line of text is indented in the original, it should be typed as near as possible to its original position. If a long verse quotation opens with a part-line, type it so that it begins at the right place; see below for examples.

For all quotations from plays, speakers' names are given in small capitals, without final punctuation but followed by a long space (or em-space). For quotations from prose plays, second and subsequent lines of a speech are indented. Stage directions within a line of text are set in italic type within roman parentheses. If a stage direction immediately follows a speaker's name, the space preceding the text is placed at the end of the stage direction, after the closing parenthesis. Stage directions which occupy a line on their own are indented further than the text, and set in italic type without parentheses. No extra space is inserted between speakers. Thus for example:

BRASSBOUND   It will teach other scoundrels to respect widows and orphans. Do you forget that there is such a thing as justice?
LADY CICELY (*gaily shaking out the finished coat*)   Oh, if you are going to dress yourself in ermine and call yourself Justice, I give you up. You are just your uncle over again; only he gets £5000 a year for it, and you do it for nothing.
She holds the coat up to see whether any further repairs are needed.
BRASSBOUND (*sulkily*)   You twist my words very cleverly.
(*Captain Brassbound's Conversion*, II)

In verse quotations, the speakers' names are positioned to the left of the text:

MACBETH   (*aside*)   Glamis, and Thane of Cawdor:
The greatest is behind. — Thanks for your pains.
(*To Banquo*)   Do you not hope your children shall be kings,
When those that gave the Thane of Cawdor to me,
Promised no less to them?
BANQUO   That trusted home
Might yet enkindle you unto the crown,
Besides the Thane of Cawdor.
(*Macbeth*, I. 3. 117–23)

§2.16. Footnote and Endnote Numbers

(a) The reference number

Wherever possible, a note reference number should be placed at the end of a sentence. Notes should be marked in the typescript by superior (superscript) numbers, in sequence throughout an article or chapter. A note reference number should follow any punctuation (including a parenthesis) except a dash, which it should precede. It should appear at the end of a quotation, not following the author's name if that precedes the quotation.

After a comma,[13] not after a dash[14] — but after a full stop.[15] F. M. L. Thompson describes footnotes as a 'parade of attribution, exegesis, and qualification'.[16]

Do not attach a note number to a heading or subheading; an asterisk may, however, be used to indicate a general note to an entire chapter. Nor should a note number (or, indeed, an asterisk) be attached to the title of an article; a note attached to the first or last sentence, or an unnumbered note preceding the numbered ones, is preferable.

(b) The text of the note

All notes, even if they are partial sentences, should be punctuated as complete sentences. For example:

[22] As seen also in Canto II of *Childe Harold's Pilgrimage*.

[13] Ibid., p. 28.

If possible, do not begin a note with an abbreviation which is normally printed in lower-case characters ('e.g.', 'i.e.', 'pp.'). If this cannot be avoided, note that 'c.', 'e.g.', 'i.e.', 'l.', 'll.', 'p.', and 'pp.' remain entirely in lower case:

[21] e.g. in July 1841.

Other abbreviations, such as 'cf.' or 'ibid.', take an initial capital at the start of a note. See also §7.12 on the use of 'ibid.'.

3 • Capitalization and Italicization

Rules on capitalization and italicization are in one sense straightforward: after all, a word is either capitalized or not and either italicized or not. But since each publisher has a slightly different set of conventions for these typographical features, the MHRA has to set out its preferences and ask authors to follow its choices. It is hoped that the following chapter clears up most common issues encountered. In the case of capitalization in particular, your software's automatic spellchecker may prove misleading, and it is always worth checking its suggestions against the rules set out here.

§3.1. When to Capitalize

Capitals must be used for the initial letters of sentences and for the names of places, persons, nationalities, the days of the week, and months (but not for the seasons of the year). They are also to be used for the titles of laws, plans (such as the Marshall Plan), wars, treaties, legal cases, and for specific institutions and other organizations (the Modern Humanities Research Association, the Poetry Book Club). Capitals are used also for unique events and periods (the Flood, the Iron Age, the Peasants' Revolt, the Reformation, the Enlightenment, the French Revolution, World War II, the Last Judgement) and for parts of books when referred to specifically (Chapter 9, Appendix A, Figure 8, Part 11).

Names of the points of the compass are capitalized only when abbreviated (N.) or when they indicate a specific area (the North [of England], South America) or a political concept (the West, the Global South). The corresponding adjectives are capitalized when they are part of an official name (Northern Ireland) or when they refer to political concepts rather than merely to geographical areas (Western Europe) but not otherwise (northern England).

'Middle' is capitalized in such fixed expressions as Middle East(ern), Middle Ages, Middle English.

Words used to describe cultural or ethnic groups, for example, Black, Native American, Latina, Jewish, and Lutheran, are generally capitalized. White is not normally capitalized, but there may be contexts where this is appropriate for consistency.

Adjectives deriving from proper nouns are in many cases not capitalized (but see §3.3):

> Alps, alpine; Bible, biblical; Satan, satanic (but Satanic with reference to Satan himself)

Dictionaries and style guides vary in their use of capitals or lower case for adjectives, verbs, and nouns deriving from names of peoples or languages. MHRA practice is to use capitals in such cases:

> Francophile, Gallicism, Italianist, Latinate

Whereas MHRA does not use capitals for:

> anglicize, anglophone, francophone, romanization

MHRA writes 'arabic numerals' and 'roman type' in lower case, but 'the Arabic language' and 'the Roman alphabet' with a capital.

§3.2. Capitalizing Personal Titles and Positions

Capitals are used for titles and positions when these appear in full or immediately preceding a personal name, or when they are used specifically, but not otherwise:

> The Archbishop of Canterbury and several other bishops were present, but Bishop Treweek was not.
> The Prime Minister met with several ministers, including the Minister for Health.

When, after a first full reference, or with such reference understood, a title is used incompletely but still with specific application to an individual, the capital is retained:

> The Archbishop spoke first.

A word or phrase used as a substitute for, or an extension of, a personal name also takes initial capitals:

> the Iron Duke
> Alfred the Great
> the Dark Lady of the Sonnets

§3.3. Capitalizing Movements and Periods

Capitals must be used for nouns and adjectives denoting cultural, philosophical, literary, critical, and artistic movements and periods when these are derived from proper nouns:

> Beauvoirian, Cartesian, Chomskyan, Christian, Confucian, Freudian, Platonism

Capitals should also be used for movements whose names are relatively rarely discussed (Vorticism, Symbolism, Futurist) or which might be open to misinterpretation if written without capitals (Decadence, Romantic, Realist). For example:

> a poet of the Romantic school
> a novel with a straightforwardly romantic plot

Lower case may be used for movements whose names have entered the language (modernist, nihilist, surrealist, communism). A degree of common sense is required; for instance, if discussing a number of movements alongside one another, it may be preferable to treat them all the same way. In all cases, make sure your usage is consistent.

Capitals should similarly be used for words such as Conservative, Democrat(ic), Independent, Liberal, National(ist), Republican, or Social(ist) where they occur in the names of political parties or affiliations, but not where they are used less specifically:

> the Independent Labour Party
> the Liberal Democrats
> standing as an Independent
> a person of conservative views
> an economic liberal

For movements and periods with the prefix 'neo' and other compounds, see §3.5.

§3.4. Capitalizing Titles of Works

In most modern European languages except English and French, and in Latin and transliterated Slavonic languages, capitalization in the titles of books, series, articles, essays, poems, films, plays, etc. follows the rules of capitalization in normal prose. That is, the first word and all proper nouns

(in German all nouns) take an initial capital, and all other words take a lower-case initial:
> *La vida es sueño*
> *El alcalde de Zalamea*
> *Il seme sotto la neve*
> *De senectute*
> *Autorenlexikon der deutschen Gegenwartsliteratur*
> 'Salazar: o homem e a sua obra'
> *Atlante dei canzonieri in volare del Quattrocento*

In English titles, the initial letters of the first word and of all nouns, pronouns (except the relative 'that'), adjectives, verbs, adverbs, and subordinating conjunctions are capitalized, but those of articles, possessive determiners ('my', etc.), prepositions, and the co-ordinating conjunctions 'and', 'but', 'or', and 'nor' are not:

> books:
>> *Put Out More Flags*
>> *How Far Can You Go?*
>> *The Man Who Was Thursday*
>> *All's Well that Ends Well*
>> *Pride and Prejudice*
>> *A Voyage towards the South Pole*
>
> series:
>> A Social History of the Welsh Language
>
> poems:
>> *The Faerie Queene*
>> 'The Passionate Shepherd to his Love'

If a poem has no title, the first line may be used to identify it. In this case, capitalization follows the author's choices:
> 'As kingfishers catch fire, dragonflies draw flame'
> '"next to of course god america i"'

In early modern studies it is common practice to follow the capitalization of the original title page, but care should be taken when copying the title of an early printed book from a database, as the database may transcribe a title that was in full capitals on the title page into all lower case. Consult the original title page for correct capitalization, where possible. If this does not resolve the issue, standardize to modern capitalization rather than leaving the title in lower case.

English works with foreign titles are normally capitalized according to the English convention rather than that of the language of the title:

Religio Medici

'Portrait d'une Femme'

'La Figlia che Piange'

In French titles it is normally only the initial letters of the first word and of proper nouns that are capitalized. But if the first word is a definite article, the following noun and any preceding adjectives also take an initial capital:

Le Médecin malgré lui

Les Grands Cimetières sous la lune

Un début dans la vie

Une ténébreuse affaire

Du latin aux langues romanes

Nouveau cours de grammaire

Histoire de la littérature française

A la recherche du temps perdu

'Edmond de Goncourt et les Naturalistes belges dans les années 1880'

However, for reasons of symmetry, capitals are sometimes used elsewhere:

'Le Corbeau et le Renard'

Le Rouge et le Noir

Titles consisting of a complete sentence (and that begin with a definite article) do not take additional capitals:

Les dieux ont soif

La guerre de Troie n'aura pas lieu

Where a work has a subtitle, the use of capitals or lower case for the first word after the colon varies between languages.

In English and in German, the first word of a subtitle following a colon is capitalized:

A 'New' Woman in Verga and Pirandello: From Page to Stage

Critical Race Theory: The Key Writings that Formed the Movement

'Exil in der Literatur: Zwischen Metapher und Realität'

Note that MHRA style separates a title from a subtitle with a colon, in preference to the full stop that is the norm in some other languages.

In English, where *or* introduces an alternative title after a semi-colon, it is set in lower case, while any article that follows it is capitalized:

> *All for Love; or, The World Well Lost*
> *Frankenstein; or, The Modern Prometheus*

In other languages, lower case is used for the first word after a colon:

> 'Uma edição fac-similada d'*Os Lusíadas*, 1572: o caso das páginas trocadas'
>
> 'Un canzoniere adespoto di Mariotto Davanzati: metrica e filologia attributiva'
>
> *Rubén Darío: cosmopolita arraigado*
>
> 'Monstruosité de l'héroine: réécriture de Médée dans *Chanson douce* de Leïla Slimani'
>
> 'Zhyvi mertsi: shche kil′ka notatok pro smert′ ukraïns′koï literatury'

Beyond the first word after the colon, subtitles are capitalized in the same way as titles, in all languages.

Capitalization in the titles of newspapers and journals is inconsistent. In particular, in Romance languages, initials of some or all nouns and adjectives are sometimes capitalized, e.g.:

> *Le Bien Public, Il Corriere della Sera, Dernières Nouvelles d'Alsace, El País, La Repubblica, Revue de Linguistique Romane*

The safest procedure is to adopt the preferred style of each publication.

§3.5. Compounds

Capitals should be retained after the prefix in hyphenated compound forms such as:

> neo-Aristotelian, non-Christian, post-Darwinian, post-Impressionism, pre-Columbian

Both parts of the compound are capitalized in 'Pre-Raphaelite'.

The following unhyphenated forms, uncapitalized or capitalized as shown, are preferred:

> neoclassical, neocolonial, neorealism, neoscholastic, Neoplatonism, Nonconformism, Presocratic

Archaeologists and historians, when referring to prehistoric eras, usually write them as one word, capitalized when a noun but not when an adjective:

> before the Neolithic, neolithic sites

In titles and headings, all parts of the compound are normally capitalized:

>   Anglo-Jewish Studies
>   Non-Christian Communities
>   Seventeenth-Century Music
>   Post-Classical Literature

However, only the prefix is capitalized if both parts are essentially one word in hyphenated compounds formed with *re-*:

>   Democracy Re-established

§3.6. Accents on Capitals

Accents should be retained on capitals in languages other than English, e.g.:

>   le Moyen Âge, Éire, el Éufrates, Émile Zola, Ólafsson

However, the French preposition *à* may drop the accent when capitalized (*A bientôt!*).

§3.7. Italicizing Words

(a) English words

Avoid the use of italics for rhetorical emphasis. Any word or phrase individually discussed should, however, be in italics, and any interpretation of it in single quotation marks:

>   He glosses *pale* as 'fenced land, park'.

It may also be desirable to use italics to distinguish one word or phrase from another, as, for example, in '23 April *not* 23rd April'.

(b) Foreign words

Single words or short phrases in foreign languages (e.g. *fin de siècle*) not used as direct quotations should be in italics. Direct, acknowledged, or more substantial quotations should be in roman type. (For quotation style, see §2.12.)

Names of institutions, buildings, towns, or regions should not be italicized, but names of movements or other abstractions should be. For example, Bibliothèque nationale de France, but *aménagement du territoire*.

Foreign words and phrases which have passed into regular English usage should not be italicized, though the decision between italic and roman type may sometimes be a fine one. In doubtful instances it is usually best to use roman. The following are examples of words which are no longer italicized:

a literary salon, ad hoc, avant-garde, denouement, dilettante, ennui, feng shui, leitmotif, milieu, par excellence, résumé, schadenfreude

Certain Latin words and abbreviations which are in common English usage are also no longer italicized. For example:

cf., e.g., etc., ibid., i.e., passim, viz.

Exceptions are made of the Latin *sic*, frequently used within quotations (see §2.8) and therefore conveniently differentiated by the use of italic, and of *circa* (abbreviated as *c*., see §5.1).

See also §7.12 on the use of 'ibid.' and similar abbreviations.

§3.8. Italicizing Titles of Works

(a) Books and other writings

Italics are used for the titles of all works individually published under their own titles: books, journals, plays, longer poems, pamphlets, and any other entire published work.

Alfred Jarry's *Ubu Roi*
T. S. Eliot's *The Waste Land*
Marx's and Engels's *The Communist Manifesto*

However, titles such as 'the Bible', 'the Koran', and 'the Talmud' are printed in roman, as are titles of books of the Bible (see below). Titles of series are not italicized, e.g. 'Studies in Hispanic and Lusophone Cultures'. The titles of chapters in books or of articles in books or journals should be in roman type enclosed within single quotation marks. The titles of poems, short stories, or essays which form part of a larger volume or other whole, or the first lines of poems used as titles, should also be given in roman type in single quotation marks:

Théophile Gautier's 'L'Art'
Keats's 'Ode on a Grecian Urn'
Shelley's 'Music, when soft voices die'
Rossetti's 'Goblin Market'
Bacon's 'Of Superstition'
Hughes's 'Harlem'

The titles of collections of manuscripts should be given in roman type without quotation marks (see §7.7). The titles of unpublished theses should be given in roman type in single quotation marks (see §7.10).

Titles of other works which appear within an italicized title should be printed in italics and enclosed within single quotation marks:

> *An Approach to 'Hamlet'*

In the citation of legal cases the names of the contending parties and 'v.' for 'versus' are given in italics:

> *Bardell v. Pickwick*
> *Roe v. Wade*

(b) Films, music, and works of art

Titles of films, substantial musical compositions, and works of art are italicized:

> *The Great Dictator*
> *Il trovatore*
> *Elijah*
> *Swan Lake*
> Beethoven's *Eroica* Symphony
> *Tapiola*
> *Die schöne Müllerin*
> *Goyescas*
> *The Hay Wain*
> *The Laughing Cavalier*
> Hambling's *Scallop*
> *A Love Supreme*
> Fleetwood Mac's *Rumours*

Descriptive or numerical titles such as the following, however, take neither italics (except in a reference to a publication or recording: see §7.8) nor quotation marks:

> Beethoven's Third Symphony
> Bach's Mass in B minor
> Mendelssohn's Andante and Scherzo
> Piano Concerto no. 1 in B flat minor

Titles of songs and other short individual pieces (like those of poems) are given in roman and within single quotation marks:

'Who is Sylvia?'
'La Marseillaise'
'Mercury, the Winged Messenger' from Holst's *The Planets*
'I Am the Walrus' from the album *Magical Mystery Tour*

(c) Exhibitions

Titles of exhibitions should be given in roman type and in single quotation marks:

'Dürer's Journeys: Travels of a Renaissance Artist'
'Barbara Hepworth: Art and Life'

(d) Italics in translated titles

If it is helpful to your reader to translate the foreign-language title of a work, place the English version in brackets after the original.

There may be instances where it is useful to distinguish between the title under which a work was published, broadcast, or distributed abroad (which should be italicized as for the original) and your literal translation of a work that has either not been translated or has been published under a different name in translation. In this case, give the title in roman type:

L'amica geniale (*My Brilliant Friend*)
L'Aigle à deux têtes (*The Eagle with Two Heads*)
Engrenages (*Spiral*) is credited with launching the career of [...]
Engrenages (Gears) set out to show the inner mechanics of the judicial system. Broadcast in the UK as *Spiral*, it [...]

The publication you are writing for may require round or square brackets as standard for translations: here we have used round. See §2.8.

4 • Names

This chapter sets out our practice for the spelling and use of proper names, where there might be uncertainty or variation. For examples beyond those given here, the 'New Oxford Dictionary for Writers and Editors' may be of assistance. Geographical name changes are generally well recorded in online encyclopaedias.

§4.1. Place Names

(a) Historical forms

In a historical context, relevant anglicized or obsolete names may be appropriate (e.g. *Bombay, Danzig, Rhodesia*), but otherwise current usage should be respected (e.g. *Mumbai, Gdańsk, Zimbabwe*).

(b) Anglicized forms

Where there is a current English form for foreign place names, it should be used:

> Brussels, Cologne, Dunkirk, Florence, Geneva, Lisbon, Majorca, Mexico City, Moscow, Munich, Naples, Quebec, Salonika, Turin, Venice, Vienna

The forms *Luxembourg, Lyon, Marseille, Reims,* and *Strasbourg* are now more widely used than *Luxemburg, Lyons, Marseilles, Rheims,* and *Strasburg* or *Strassburg* and are therefore recommended.

Where countries have officially changed the English-language spelling of towns and cities (for instance, from *Calcutta* to *Kolkata* or from *Kiev* to *Kyiv*) this is to be respected, though it may be necessary to use the historical version in writing about the past (e.g. *Danzig* rather than *Gdańsk* in an analysis of Günter Grass's *The Danzig Trilogy*). The same applies to country names: respect the currently accepted designation (for instance, *Myanmar*) but use the historical name where appropriate to the context (for instance, *Burma* when analysing Orwell's *Burmese Days*).

The definite article is no longer used in the names of the countries *Lebanon, Sudan,* and *Ukraine* (but *the Gambia, the Netherlands*).

The following are now the official spellings of certain Welsh names (including in texts written in English) and should be used instead of the anglicized forms found in earlier maps and books:

> Aberdyfi, Aberystwyth, Betws-y-Coed, Caernarfon, Conwy (river and town), Dolgellau, Ffestiniog, Llanelli, Tywyn

(c) Punctuation in place names

The use or non-use of hyphens in names such as *Newcastle upon Tyne*, *Stratford-upon-Avon* should be checked in a good reference work. French place names are regularly hyphenated, e.g. *Colombey-les-Deux-Églises*, *Châlons-sur-Marne, Saint-Malo*, except for an introductory definite article, e.g. *Le Havre, Les Baux-de-Provence*.

(d) Parts of the British Isles

Note the difference between (a) Great Britain (England, Scotland, Wales), (b) the United Kingdom (England, Scotland, Wales, Northern Ireland), (c) the British Isles (England, Scotland, Wales, Ireland, the Isle of Man, the Channel Islands). In particular, note:

> that *England* should never be used for any of the above;
> that in the context of the nation state in the present day, the term *United Kingdom* should be used;
> that the Irish form *Éire* should not be used in English as the name of the Republic of Ireland;
> that the Isle of Man and the Channel Islands are not parts of England, of Great Britain, or of the United Kingdom.

§4.2. Academic Institutions

Care needs to be taken to ensure that the names of academic institutions are correctly given, e.g. *Johns Hopkins University* (not *John*), *Magdalen College* (Oxford), *Magdalene College* (Cambridge). Universities and colleges with similar names must be clearly distinguished, such as the *University of Pennsylvania* and *Penn State University*, the *University of York* (England) and *York University* (Toronto).

§4.3. Personal Names

(a) Classical names

Where generally accepted English forms of classical names exist (*Horace, Livy, Ptolemy, Virgil*), they should be used.

(b) Popes and saints

Names of popes and saints should normally be given in their English form (*Gregory, Innocent, Paul, St Francis of Assisi, St John of the Cross*). In a philosophical or historical context, the title 'St' may be omitted (*Thomas Aquinas, Augustine of Hippo*).

(c) Kings and queens

Names of foreign kings and queens should normally be given in their English form where one exists (*Charles V, Catherine the Great, Ferdinand and Isabella, Francis I, Henry IV, Victor Emmanuel*). Those names for which no English form exists (*Haakon, Sancho*) or for which the English form is quaint or archaic (*Alphonse, Lewis* for *Alfonso, Louis*) should retain their foreign form. If in the course of a work it is necessary to refer to some monarchs whose names have acceptable English forms and some which do not, in the interests of consistency it is better to use the foreign form for all:

> the reigns of Fernando III and Alfonso X
> Henri IV was succeeded by Louis XIII

For when to capitalize titles such as 'duke' or 'queen', see §3.2.

(d) Non-English names

A comprehensive reference work for global naming conventions is:

> *Names of Persons: National Usage for Entries in Catalogues* (International Federation of Library Associations, 1996) <https://www.ifla.org/files/assets/cataloguing/pubs/names-of-persons_1996.pdf> [accessed 10 May 2023]

The following brief notes cover some of the most common issues arising in practice:

Celtic. Care must be taken over the spelling of Celtic names in *Mc, Mac,* etc. (e.g. *McDonald, MacDonald, M'Donald, Macmillan, Mac Liammóir*); adopt the form used by the individual in question.

Distinguish between Irish names that retain their original form (*Ó Máille*) and those that are anglicized (*O'Donnell*).

Note that *ap* and *ab*, in Welsh names such as Llywelyn ap Madog, are neither capitalized nor hyphenated.

Dutch and Flemish. Surnames in *van* take a lower-case initial in the Netherlands (*van der Plas, van Toorn*) but are generally capitalized in Belgium (*Van den Bremt, Van Ryssel*).

French. In case of ambiguity concerning the correct spelling of names of French authors, use as a guide the catalogue of the Bibliothèque nationale de France (<https://www.bnf.fr/>).

Slavonic. Names originally written in a non-Latin script (e.g. Достоевский) should be given in transliterated form (e.g. Dostoevsky). It is important that this be done consistently, following a scholarly scheme: see §1.2 (f).

For the alphabetization of names, see §8.1 and §8.2.

(e) Initials

Use initials for forenames only if authors or artists publish in this form or are widely known by this form of their name. Follow each initial with a full stop and a space. For instance:

> C. P. E. Bach, T. S. Eliot, E. T. A. Hoffmann, J. K. Rowling

§4.4. Possessives of Personal Names

The possessive of personal names ending in a pronounced -*s* or -*z* is formed in the normal way by adding an apostrophe and *s*:

> Berlioz's symphonies, Cervantes's works, Ta-Nehisi Coates's essays, Dickens's characters, bell hooks's theories, in Inigo Jones's day, Dylan Thomas's use of language

French names ending in an unpronounced -*s*, -*x*, or -*z* also follow the normal rule and take an apostrophe and *s*:

> Cixous's criticism, Descartes's works, Malraux's style, Cherbuliez's novels

The possessive of names ending in -*us* also conforms to the normal rule:

> Claudius's successor, Herodotus's *Histories*, Jesus's parables, an empire greater than Darius's

However, the possessive of *Moses* and of Greek names ending in -*es* (particularly those having more than two syllables) is usually formed by means of the apostrophe alone:

under Moses' leadership, Demosthenes' speeches, Sophocles' plays, Xerxes' campaigns

5 • Dates, Numbers, and Quantities

Dates, numbers, and quantities can be set out in various ways and there is considerable variation between publishers. This chapter sets out the MHRA's conventions.

§5.1. Dates

Dates should be given in the form '23 April 1564'. The name of the month should always appear in full between the day ('23' *not* '23rd' or '23rd') and the year. No internal punctuation should be used except when a day of the week is mentioned, e.g. 'Friday, 12 October 2001'.

When referring to a period of time, use the form 'between 1826 and 1850' or 'from 1826 to 1850' (*not* 'between 1826–50' or 'from 1826–50'), 'from January to March 1970' (*not* 'from January–March 1970').

Dating systems used before the modern age require special conventions. If it is necessary to refer to a date in both Old and New Styles, the form '11/21 July 1605' should be used. For dates dependent upon the time of beginning the new year, the form '21 January 1564/5' should be used.

In citations of the era, 'BC', 'BCE', 'CE', and 'AH' follow the year and 'AD' precedes it, and small capitals without full stops are used:

> 54 BC, 54 BCE, 622 CE, 1 AH, AD 622

With reference to centuries, all of these, including 'AD', follow:

> in the third century BC

In references to decades, an *s* without an apostrophe should be used:

> the 1920s (*not* the 1920's)
> the 60s

In references to centuries the ordinal should be spelled out:

> the sixteenth century (*not* the 16th century)
> sixteenth-century drama

In giving approximate dates *circa* should be abbreviated as *c.* followed by a space:

> *c.* 1490, *c.* 300 BC

§5.2. Numbers

Numbers up to and including one hundred, including ordinals, should be written in words when the context is not statistical. Figures should be used for volume, part, chapter, and page numbers:

> Chapter 3 discusses Part II of Mahler's Symphony no. 8.
>
> The second chapter is longer than the first.

Figures are also used for years, including those below one hundred (see §5.1), and for ages of people:

> At the age of 45, Julius Caesar invaded Britain, landing in 55 BCE.

However, numbers at the beginning of sentences and approximate numbers should be expressed in words, as should 'hundred', 'thousand', 'million', 'billion', etc., if they appear as whole numbers:

> Two hundred and forty-seven pages were written.
>
> The fire destroyed about five thousand books.
>
> She lived and wrote a thousand years ago.

Words should be preferred to figures where inelegance would otherwise result:

> He asked for ninety soldiers and received nine hundred and ninety.

In expressing inclusive numbers falling within the same hundred, the last two figures should be given, including any zero in the penultimate position:

> 13–15, 44–47, 100–22, 104–08, 1933–39

Where four-digit numbers do not fall within the same hundred, give both figures in full:

> 1098–1101

Date spans before the Common Era (BCE) should be stated in full since the shorter form could be misleading:

> The First Punic War (264–241 BCE) (*not* 264–41 BCE)

Numbers up to 9999 are written without a comma, e.g. 2589; those from 10,000 upwards take a comma, e.g. 125,397; those with seven or more digits take two or more commas, separating groups of three digits counting from the right, e.g. 9,999,000,000. However, where digits align in columns, e.g. in tables or accounts, commas must be consistently included or omitted in all numbers above 999.

§5.3. Roman Numerals

The use of roman numerals should be confined to a few specific purposes:

(a) large capitals for the ordinals of monarchs, popes, etc. (Edward VII), and for major events customarily written with roman numerals: World War II, Superbowl LII, Vatican II;

(b) small capitals for volume numbers of books (journals and series use arabic numerals), also for the acts of plays, for 'books' or other major subdivisions of long poems, novels, etc. (see §7.3 (c));

(c) small capitals for centuries in some languages other than English ('xvie siècle', 'siglo xvii'); however, in Cyrillic script large capitals are used;

(d) lower case for the preliminary pages of a book or journal (even if the original uses capitals), where these are numbered separately; inclusive numbers are written out in full, e.g. 'xxiv–xxviii' *not* 'xxiv–viii'.

§5.4. Currency

Words should be used to express simple sums of money occurring in normal prose:

> The manuscript was sold for eight shillings in 1865.
> The reprint costs twenty-five pounds or thirty euros.
> The fee was three hundred francs.
> He was paid twenty roubles.

Names of foreign currencies, including the pre-2002 European currencies, should be given in their English form where one is in common use, e.g. 'mark' or 'deutschmark' (*not* 'deutsche Mark'). Note, too, the use of English plurals such as 'drachmas', 'pfennigs' (*but* 'Italian lire').

Sums of money which are awkward to express in words, or sums occurring in statistical tables, etc., may be written in figures. British currency before 1971 should be shown in the following form:

> The manuscript was sold for £197 12s. 6d. in 1965.

Sums in modern currencies are given as follows:

> €250, $500, $8.95, 25c, ¥2000, £12.95, 35p, 20 roubles

Where it is necessary to specify that reference is being made to the American, Canadian, or some other dollar, an appropriate abbreviation precedes the symbol without a full stop or a space:

US$, C$ (*or* Can$), A$ (*or* Aus$), NZ$

Unless writing in a historical context, avoid traditional abbreviations such as 'kr.' for the Danish, Swedish, or Norwegian krone/krona, and instead write the modern currency codes 'NOK', 'DKK', or 'SEK', before the figure and separated from it by a space, e.g. 'SEK 120'. Similarly for the Swiss franc, 'CHF'.

Of the European currencies replaced by the euro in 2002, abbreviations for the Belgian franc, 'BF', French franc, 'F', and Spanish peseta, 'Pt' or 'Pts', should be written after the figure: '670 Pts'. The deutschmark, however, precedes it (and is separated from it by a space): 'DM 8'.

§5.5. Weights and Measures

In non-statistical contexts express weights and measures in words:

> He bought a phial of laudanum and an ounce of arsenic at a pharmacy two miles from Cheapside.

In statistical works or in subjects where frequent reference is made to them, weights and measures may be expressed in figures with appropriate abbreviations, with a space between the figure and the abbreviation:

> The priory is situated 3 km from the village of Emshall.
> The same 13 mm capitals were used by three Madrid printers at different times.

Note that most such abbreviations do not take a full stop or plural *s*:

> 1 kg, 15 kg, 1 mm, 6 cm, 15 m, 4 l (litres), 2 ft, 100 lb, 10 oz

But, to avoid ambiguity, use 'in.' for 'inch(es)'.

6 • DOIs and URLs

> *Academic writing almost always involves making reference to digital resources. Articles in scholarly journals are now always assigned DOIs, while discussions of contemporary artists or authors often involve quoting from interviews published only on websites, which must be referenced by URL. Academic writers therefore need to be able to cite DOIs and URLs, and this chapter describes how to write each in MHRA style. This is not a chapter on 'how to reference digital resources': for the most part, digital resources should be referenced very similarly to printed resources, as Chapter 7 on Referencing discusses.*

§6.1. The Difference between a DOI and a URL

Both DOIs and URLs are ways to identify digital resources, but they work in different ways and cover different things. URLs are like addresses, saying on which web page something can be found. Because the web is constantly changing, with new websites appearing and disappearing, and existing websites going through internal rearrangements, URLs cannot be relied on to remain accurate over time. All that can really be said is that something was at a given page on a given date; it may or may not still be there today. As a result, URLs must always be cited with an access date: see below. Another issue with URLs is that the same content may be available from multiple locations. It is sometimes unclear what the best address for a resource is.

DOIs, by contrast, are permanent identification numbers for digital resources, in the same way that ISBNs provide permanent ID numbers for editions. Once allocated, these never change. It is customary now for each individual article, and even each short book review, in a scholarly journal to be allocated its own DOI. Many articles have been retrospectively allocated DOIs: *Modern Language Review*, for example, has DOIs going back to its foundation in 1905. DOIs are also sometimes given to specific entries in large online encyclopaedias. They are not confined to scholarly work or to commercial electronic publishing: governmental papers can also be given them (so, for example, many OECD, European Union, or HMSO publications have DOIs).

§6.2. How to Format a DOI

As is standard for abbreviations, the term 'DOI' is capitalized when discussing its role and use. In notation of an individual DOI, however, the letters are set in lower case followed by a colon ('doi:'), followed immediately, and without a space, by the identifier itself, a series of alphanumeric codes broken up by slashes and colons. For example:

> Frank A. J. L. James, 'Faraday, Michael (1791–1867), Natural Philosopher, Scientific Adviser, and Sandemanian', *Dictionary of National Biography* (Oxford University Press, entry dated 2004, rev. 2011), doi:10.1093/ref:odnb/9153

> Els Jongeneel, 'Art and Divine Order in the *Divina Commedia*', *Literature and Theology*, 21 (2007), pp. 131–45, doi:10.1093/litthe/frm008

Do not give an access date, and do not write a DOI in angle brackets. Do not convert DOIs into URL form to produce a reference such as:

> Els Jongeneel, 'Art and Divine Order in the *Divina Commedia*', *Literature and Theology*, 21 (2007), pp. 131–45 <https://doi.org/10.1093/litthe/frm008> [accessed 11 May 2023]

§6.3. How to Format a URL

Web addresses should be written in angle brackets. Inside those brackets, URLs almost always begin 'https://'; this is part of the URL and must be included. For example:

> <https://www.mhra.org.uk> [accessed 17 November 2023]

An inconvenience of URLs is that addresses for individual pages inside large websites can be very long, and subject to change without notice as those websites go through periodic redesigns. Because of this, access dates must always be given when citing a URL: this is the date on which you, as the author, made use of the contents of the page. (Internet services such as the Wayback Machine sometimes allow pages dropped by their original hosts to be rediscovered, and an access date is invaluable in such cases.) It is good practice to recheck your URLs just before submitting a book or article to a publisher, to see if the material is still where you say it is: if so, you can then update the access date. If the page you are citing is of a kind where the published text is likely to change over time, it is important to check that the information or words you have cited remain the same. If not, retain your original access date.

Another good practice is to cite URLs in the shortest and friendliest form possible. The same page is often reachable by multiple URLs. If a website describes a URL as a 'permalink', this means it aspires to be a permanent location: blog engines such as WordPress often provide these. If available, use a permalink. For example:

> <https://www.mhra.org.uk/news/2023/01/09/into-the-vernacular.html> [accessed 25 April 2023]

The 'share' option on a web page may provide a permalink. While shorter forms are generally preferable, avoid quoting URLs from services such as tinyurl or bitly which abbreviate other URLs: quote the originals.

Where the page to be cited is deep inside a website intended to be accessed by searching and not by URLs, it is sometimes appropriate to give just a page title and the URL for the site itself. For example, to refer to the entry 'locator' in the *OED*, format the note as follows:

> See the entry 'locator' in *Oxford English Dictionary*, n.d., <https://www.oed.com> [accessed 25 April 2023]

The short form is more helpful to future scholars, since the *OED* website is likely to change its internal organization and URLs every few years.

When providing a URL for an entry in an online catalogue or database is unavoidable, there are ways in which it can be shortened. URLs often seem long because of the use of a '?' and subsequent '&...' details. For example:

> <https://www.imdb.com/title/tt0078748/?pf_rd_m=A2FGELUUNOQJNL&pf_rd_p=1a264172-ae11-42e4-8ef7-7fed1973bb8f&pf_rd_r=AZSF34JS4W2CP2RR0KBC&pf_rd_s=center-1&pf_rd_t=15506&pf_rd_i=top&ref_=chttp_tt_52> [accessed 13 May 2023]

In almost all cases, those additional details are spurious as far as identification goes, since they are part of the website's tracking data. (In this case, the film *Alien* has been accessed via a list of the top 250 movies in the Internet Movie Database.) The same page can be reached if everything from the question mark onwards is deleted:

> <https://www.imdb.com/title/tt0078748> [accessed 13 June 2023]

Similarly, a database may include your own search terms in the URL that is visible in its address bar. A search in the Internet Movie Database for *Portrait of a Lady on Fire* produces the URL:

> <https://www.imdb.com/title/tt8613070/?ref_=nv_sr_srsg_1_tt_7_nm_0_q_portrait%2520of%2520a%2520lady%2520on%2520fire>

This can be shortened to the core URL:

<https://www.imdb.com/title/tt8613070>

Though we strive to quote short URLs, they often still look lengthy on the page. When submitting a URL as part of word-processed copy, do not include line breaks or hyphenation, however ugly the result: leave it to the typesetter to deal with.

If a document such as a newspaper article is accessed through a database, via a library login, the search may produce what looks like a URL in the address line but is in fact a record of the search within the system, to which only fellow users of that library have access. Such internal locators typically contain the name of the database and a code for the library. In such cases, best practice is to locate the original source online and give its URL. If this is not possible, do not give a URL.

7 • References

This has always been the most frequently consulted chapter of the Style Guide, as it sets out the format for referencing a writer's sources. 'MHRA style' has traditionally been understood to mean citing sources in footnotes or endnotes. Accordingly, the conventions for setting these out are dealt with thoroughly, covering as many likely source genres as is possible in a compact guide. At the same time, the MHRA has for many years also published works that use author–date referencing. Conventions for this system are also explained here and in the following chapter.

The word 'note' is used throughout as an umbrella term for footnotes and endnotes, which share the same format regardless of their placement on the page. While the examples in this chapter show the material to be included in a note, they are not set out as notes — with a superscript footnote number and left justification — since notes are created and set out automatically by your writing software.

§7.1. Citation in Notes vs Author–Date Citation

In academic writing, referencing generally takes one of two forms. In the first form, a source is cited in full in a note (either footnote or endnote) when first mentioned in the author's argument. In books, and occasionally also in journals, this full reference is then also listed in an alphabetical list of cited sources. In the second form of reference, generally known as author–date citation, a minimal reference is incorporated into the main text in a format that can easily be matched to the full reference, which appears in the alphabetical list of cited sources provided at the end of the article, chapter, or book. This style goes by various other names: 'in-text citation', 'parenthetical citation', or 'Harvard style'.

The *MHRA Style Guide* has always been closely associated with the first form of reference, which uses footnotes or endnotes (accompanied, in books, by a bibliography). So strong is this association that online referencing aids will often offer a choice between 'MHRA or Harvard', where Harvard is shorthand for author–date referencing.

However, the MHRA has for many years also published work in fields that conventionally use author–date referencing and offers a free choice to its book authors. We therefore present the two forms of reference on an equal footing in this chapter. Because footnote and endnote references contain complete information on the cited source, that section is much longer. The simplicity of in-text references requires little in the way of explanation. Nonetheless, since bibliographies in both systems are substantially based on the information included in a footnote or endnote, those using author–date referencing will find it useful to consult the main body of this chapter when compiling their bibliographies. See §7.13 for more on the author–date system.

§7.2. Choosing Sources

A work of literature should be quoted or referred to in a satisfactory scholarly edition, if one exists. Where there is no scholarly edition, make clear whether you are quoting the first publication of a literary work or a subsequent reprint or revised edition. If an unrevised reprint is used (such as a modern facsimile reprint of an out-of-print work or a paperback reissue of an earlier book), the publication details of the original edition as well as of the reprint should be given.

Details of original publication should also be provided where an article from a journal is reprinted in an anthology of reprinted material (see §7.3 (b)).

§7.3. Citing Books, Chapters, and Literary Works

(a) Citing entire books

Full references should be given as in the following examples of monographs (i–iii), edited volumes (iv–vi), and editions of texts (vii–xi); a commentary follows.

> (i) Priyamvada Gopal, *Insurgent Empire: Anticolonial Resistance and British Dissent* (Verso, 2020), p. 63.
>
> (ii) Essaka Joshua, *Physical Disability in British Romantic Literature* (Cambridge University Press, 2020), p. 123.
>
> (iii) Robert E. Peary, *The North Pole*, intro. by Theodore Roosevelt (Frederick A. Stokes, 1910; facsimile repr. Time Life, 1985).
>
> (iv) *Readings in the Anthropocene: The Environmental Humanities, German Studies, and Beyond*, ed. by Sabine Wilke and Japhet Johnstone (Bloomsbury, 2017), doi:10.5040/9781501307782.

(v) *Motherhood in Literature and Culture: Interdisciplinary Perspectives from Europe*, ed. by Gill Rye and others (Routledge, 2017).

(vi) *Becoming Visible: Women in European History*, ed. by Renate Bridenthal, Susan Stuard, and Merry E. Wiesner-Hanks, 3rd edn (Houghton Mifflin, 1998).

(vii) *Simone de Beauvoir: Mémoires*, ed. by Jean-Louis Jeannelle and others, 2 vols (Gallimard, 2018), II, p. 131.

(viii) Eleonora Fonseca Pimentel, *From Arcadia to Revolution: 'The Neapolitan Monitor' and Other Writings*, ed. and trans. by Verina R. Jones (Iter Press and Arizona Center for Medieval and Renaissance Studies, 2019), p. 54.

(ix) *Homeri Ilias*, ed. by Thomas W. Allen, 3 vols (Oxford University Press, 1931; facsimile repr. 2000).

(x) James Baldwin, *Collected Essays*, ed. by Toni Morrison (Library of America, 1998).

(xi) *Heinrich Böll: Werke*, ed. by Árpád Bernáth and others, Kölner Ausgabe, 27 vols (Kiepenheuer und Witsch, 2002–10), XX, *1977–79*, ed. by Jochen Schubert (2009), pp. 24–25.

The information should be given in the following order:

(1) *Author*: The author's name should normally be given as it appears on the title page; forenames should precede surnames and should not be reduced to initials. The names of up to three authors should be given in full; for works by more than three authors the name of only the first should be given, followed by 'and others' (see examples v and xi). Do not use 'et al.'. If the author's name is included within the title (as, for example, in editions of 'Works'), or if the book is an edited collection or anthology, the title will appear first (see examples iv–vii, and xi). In a footnote, treat your own name as you would anybody else's: do not use 'See my...' as a shorthand form.

(2) *Title*: The title should be given as it appears on the title page (although very long titles may be suitably abbreviated) and italicized. A colon should normally be used to separate title and subtitle, even where the punctuation on the title page is different or (as often happens) non-existent. For books in English capitalize the initial letter of the first word after the colon and of all principal words throughout the title and subtitle; for titles in other languages, follow the capitalization rules for the language in question (see §3.4). Titles of other works occurring within the title should be enclosed in quotation marks and should not be set in roman type (see example viii). For books (usually

older works) with alternative titles, punctuation before and after 'or' should be as follows:

> *The Queen; or, The Excellency of her Sex*
> *All for Love; or, The World Well Lost*

(3) *Editor, Translator, etc.*: The names of editors etc. should be treated in the same way as those of authors (as set out above) with regard to forenames and number to be given; they should be preceded by the accepted abbreviated forms 'ed. by', 'trans. by', or 'rev. by' (see examples iv–xi). If the book has an introduction or preface, give details of its author only if this information is significant (see iii). For multi-volume works where there is both a general editor and an editor for each individual volume, the information should be conveyed as in example xi. In this example, the twentieth volume of a twenty-seven-volume edition is being cited; this volume has its own editor (Jochen Schubert), and the edition as a whole has a general editorial team (Árpád Bernáth and others).

(4) *Series*: For a monograph or edited volume that is produced in a numbered series, it is not normally necessary to give the series title and number, except where this is likely to be useful to your reader. This might be the case for a multi-volume edition of an author's works, where the edition is a byword in your field (see example xi), or if it is likely that a library would file the volume under the series title. If given, series titles should not be italicized or put between quotation marks. The series number should be given in arabic numerals. For instance:

> (xii) *German Text Crimes: Writers Accused, from the 1950s to the 2000s*, ed. by Tom Cheesman, German Monitor, 77 (Rodopi, 2013).

(5) *Edition*: If the edition used is other than the first, this should be stated in the form '2nd edn', '5th edn', 'rev. edn' (see example vi). Do not use superscript for the ordinal even if your software automatically does so ('2nd' not '2nd').

(6) *Number of Volumes*: If the work is in more than one volume, the number of volumes should be given in the form '2 vols' (see examples vii, ix, and xi). Foreign equivalents, such as 'tomes', 'Bände', or 'tomos', should usually be rendered as 'vols'.

(7) *Details of Publication*: The name of the publisher and the date of publication should be enclosed in parentheses separated by a comma. While MHRA style does not require the place of publication to be given, scholars writing about the early era of printing may wish to include the place of publication of historical texts where this information is of use to readers in their field. Similarly, in some print cultures there is no publisher in the

modern sense but it may be useful to give the name of a printer, where this is known. Any detail of publication which is not given in the book itself but can be ascertained (for instance from a colophon in early books) should be enclosed in square brackets, e.g. '[Paris]', '[1787]'. For details that are assumed but uncertain, use the form '[Paris?]', '[1787?]'. If any detail is unknown and cannot be ascertained, the following abbreviated forms of reference should be used: '[n.p.]' (= no place; needed only if place of publication is being given for analogous texts), '[n. pub.]' (= no publisher), '[n.d.]' (= no date). Do not use square brackets in a reference for any other purpose (for example, when the reference is already in parentheses), otherwise the impression may be conveyed that the information in square brackets is uncertain.

The name of the publishing house should be given without secondary matter such as an initial definite article, '& Co.', 'Ltd', 'S.A.', or 'GmbH'. The words 'Press', 'Verlag', 'Editorial', etc. are usually omitted where the name of the house is that of its proprietor or founder. Do not abbreviate 'University Press' to 'UP'. Thus for example:

>Éditions de la Femme, Harvester Press, Oxford University Press, Clarendon Press, Blackwell, Mellen, Laterza, Mitteldeutscher Verlag

It is not normally necessary to include forenames or initials of publishers, unless there are two or more with the same surname:

>Brewer (*not* D. S. Brewer)
>
>Heinemann (*not* William Heinemann)
>
>Peter Lang (*to distinguish from* Herbert Lang)

A book which has been jointly published by two or more publishers should be referred to as in example viii.

Details of facsimile reprints should be given as in example ix where the original publisher is responsible for the reprint, and as in example iii where different publishers are involved.

A reference to a work in several volumes published over a period of years but now complete should state the number of volumes and give inclusive dates of publication as well as the date of the volume specifically referred to: see example xi. If a work in several volumes is still in the process of publication, the date of the first volume should be stated followed by a dash and a space, and the date of the individual volume being cited should be added in parentheses after the volume number. In some instances (for example, if each volume of a set has a different editor) it may be more appropriate to give publication details only for the volume cited.

(8) *Volume Number*: In a multi-volume work the number of the volume referred to should be given in small capital roman numerals, followed where necessary by the title and editor of the volume (if any) and by the year of publication in parentheses (see examples vii and xi).

(9) *Page Numbers*: To cite a particular point in or passage of a book, use 'p.' or 'pp.' to abbreviate 'page' or 'pages'. If an entry relates to several successive pages, the first and last page numbers of the span should always be stated:

> pp. 201–09 *not* pp. 201 ff.

Where no pagination is present (for instance in early printed books) use whatever information is present, such as signature marks or folio numbers. The abbreviated and superscript forms for 'recto' and 'verso' are preferred. For example:

> (xiii) Henry Goodcole, *The Wonderfull Discoverie of Elizabeth Sawyer a Witch, Late of Edmonton* (London: for William Butler, 1621), sig. C2^r.

Note that 'sig.' and 'fol.' are abbreviations, and thus are followed by a full stop, but the plurals 'sigs' and 'fols' are contractions, and thus are not followed by a full stop.

Referring to a position in an ebook can be difficult. Most academic ebooks are derived from an original publication which has been typeset in the traditional way, with an imprint page (giving information on the publisher and date of publication) and fixed pagination throughout. Cite as if you are citing a printed book, following the guidelines given above. There is no need to give the name of the ebook format or reader through which you accessed the work. Give page numbers or section details only if these are fixed and stable. Some ebook formats have no pagination and others give different pagination in different screen readers or formats (so that, for instance, the pagination might be different if the book is read on a phone versus on a tablet). If that is the case, do not give a page number. Instead, provide as much information as you can to enable your reader to locate the citation on any device. If you quote from the work, this should be sufficient to allow your reader to search for the location. If not quoting, consider including a chapter number or the text of a subheading.

(10) *DOI*: Some recently published books have a DOI. It is good practice to cite this if available (as in example iv).

Citations of online-only editions of authors' works should follow the rules for print books as far as possible: give as much of the information above as is available and applicable. Unless the edition is hosted at the site of a print publisher such as a university press, it may not be possible to give a publisher. In this case it is not necessary to use [n. pub.] since websites are not considered publishers for referencing purposes. However, if the edition does not specify the date(s) of its production, give [n.d.]. Where an online edition has no DOI, give a URL and access date, as for a website. For instance:

> (xiv) *Livingstone Online*, ed. by Adrian S. Wisnicki and Megan Ward (2004–21) <https://livingstoneonline.org/> [accessed 11 October 2023].

(11) In citation in notes, all citations are normally given in footnotes or endnotes rather than in the main text. An exception may be made when a large number of quotations and citations refer to a single, key text (nearly always a book). In this case, an initial footnote is used to give the publication details, establishing an abbreviated form of reference to be used thereafter, in parentheses, in the main text. Where relevant, this may include also a published translation of the text. A first footnote would take the following form (with wording adjusted to the case):

> (xv) Marcel Proust, *A la recherche du temps perdu*, ed. by Jean-Yves Tadié, 4 vols (Gallimard, 1987–89), II, p. 67, hereafter *ALR*. Subsequent references are given in parentheses in the main text.

A reference in the main text would then follow the pattern:

> The impression of the fountain when viewed 'de près' is of geometry and collage (*ALR*, III, p. 56).

An example involving a published translation would look like this:

> (xvi) Uwe Timm, *Am Beispiel meines Bruders* (Kiepenheuer und Witsch, 2003), hereafter *BmB*; translated as Uwe Timm, *In My Brother's Shadow*, trans. by Anthea Bell (Bloomsbury, 2005), hereafter *MBS*. Subsequent references are given in parentheses in the main text.

The corresponding reference in the main text would take this form:

> The narrator writes that during his childhood his older brother was 'gegenwärtiger als andere Tote' ('more present than other dead people') (*BmB*, p. 8; *MBS*, p. 2).

In a book-length study, the abbreviations may be established in a list or note in the preliminaries rather than in individual footnotes. For abbreviations of book titles see also §2.9. For the format of translated quotations see also §2.12.

(b) Citing chapters in edited collections

Full references should be given as in the following examples:

(i) Sabine Nöllgen, 'The Darkness of the Anthropocene: Wolfgang Hilbig's *Alte Abdeckerei*', in *Readings in the Anthropocene: The Environmental Humanities, German Studies, and Beyond*, ed. by Sabine Wilke and Japhet Johnstone, New Directions in German Studies, 18 (Bloomsbury, 2017), pp. 148–66 (p. 155).

(ii) Giulia Zava, 'Translating the *Canzoniere* into Images: The Petrarca Queriniano Incunable', in *Translating Petrarch's Poetry: 'L'Aura del Petrarca' from the Quattrocento to the 21st Century*, ed. by Carole Birkan-Berz, Guillaume Coatelen, and Thomas Vuong (Legenda, 2020), pp. 82–102, doi:10.2307/j.ctv16kkxw0.10.

(iii) Ani Kokobobo and Devin McFadden, 'The Queer Nihilist: Queer Time, Social Refusal, and Heteronormativity in *The Precipice*', in *Goncharov in the Twenty-First Century*, ed. by Ingrid Kleespies and Lyudmila Parts (Academic Studies Press, 2021), pp. 132–52 (pp. 146–47), doi:10.2307/j.ctv249sgs4.13.

(iv) Montserrat Lunati, 'Mercè Rodoreda and Maria-Mercè Marçal as "specters granted a hospitable memory" in Mercè Ibarz's Fiction', in *Catalan Narrative 1875–2015*, ed. by Jordi Larios and Montserrat Lunati (Legenda, 2020), pp. 139–60, doi:10.2307/j.ctv1wsgrqq.13.

When a second item from a volume previously mentioned is to be listed, use an abbreviated form of the volume details, as in this example referring to the volume in i above:

(v) Sean Ireton, 'Adalbert Stifter and the Gentle Anthropocene', in *Readings in the Anthropocene*, ed. by Wilke and Johnstone, pp. 195–221.

The bibliographical information for a chapter in a book should be given in the following order:

Author's name, exactly as it appears in the book

Title of chapter in single quotation marks

The word 'in' (preceded by a comma) followed by the collection/volume title, 'ed. by' editor's name, and full publication details of book

First and last page numbers of chapter cited, preceded by 'pp.'

Page number(s), in parentheses and preceded by 'p.' or 'pp.', of the particular reference (if necessary)

DOI. Some recently published books have DOIs. It is good practice to cite this if available (as in examples ii–iv)

A colon should be used to separate the title and subtitle of the chapter title. In cases where the author has intentionally used unusual capitalization, follow the author's preference. Otherwise, always use the following practice. For titles in English and German, capitalize the initial letter of the first word after the colon and all principal words (in German, all nouns) throughout the title (including the subtitle) (see examples); for titles in other languages, follow the capitalization rules for the language in question (see §3.4).

The titles of works of literature occurring within the titles of chapters or articles should be italicized or placed within quotation marks, whichever is appropriate (see examples i, ii, and iii). If quotation marks are used within the chapter title, they should be double (see example iv), since single quotation marks have been used to enclose the title itself.

If a particular page within a chapter is to be indicated, the full page span should be given in the first full citation and a reference to the particular page or pages added in parentheses (see examples i and iii).

Reference to an article in a book which has previously been published in a journal should take one of the following forms:

> (vi) Vicente L. Rafael, 'Translation, American English, and the National Insecurities of Empire', *Social Text*, 27.4 (2009), pp. 1–23 (repr. in *The Translation Studies Reader*, ed. by Lawrence Venuti, 4th edn (Routledge, 2021), pp. 451–68).

> (vii) Lucy O'Meara, 'Barthes and Antonioni in China: The Muffling of Criticism', in *Deliberations: The Journals of Roland Barthes*, ed. by Neil Badmington (Routledge, 2017), pp. 63–82 (first publ. in *Textual Practice*, 30.2 (2016), pp. 267–86).

When citing a single-author book, it is not generally necessary to give the title of the chapter from which you are citing. This might, however, be useful where individual chapters cover different topics and only one is relevant, provided that this information is also of use to your reader. Thus, an analysis of Annie Ernaux's prose (but not a more general analysis of autobiographical writing), might usefully give:

> (viii) Alice Blackhurst, 'Annie Ernaux: l'écriture, un luxe', in Blackhurst, *Luxury, Sensation and the Moving Image* (Legenda, 2021), pp. 55–80.

The author's surname is repeated before the book title to clarify that they are the author of both the chapter and the book.

A single poem in an anthology is cited in the same way as a chapter in a book:

> (ix) Benjamin Zephaniah, 'Dis Poetry', in Zephaniah, *City Psalms* (Bloodaxe Books, 1992), pp. 12–13.

Where a longer work such as a book-length poem or play is cited within an anthology, its title should still be italicized even though it is now part of a larger book. For example:

> (x) *Troilus and Criseyde*, in *The Riverside Chaucer*, ed. by Larry D. Benson, 3rd edn (Oxford University Press, 2008), pp. 472–585.
>
> (xi) Marqués de Santillana, *Infierno de los enamorados*, in *Poesías completas*, ed. by Miguel Ángel Pérez Priego, 2 vols (Alhambra, 1975–77), I (1975), pp. 225–58.
>
> (xii) *Livingstone's 'Missionary Travels' Manuscript*, ed. by Justin D. Livingstone and Adrian S. Wisnicki, rev. edn (2020), in *Livingstone Online*, ed. by Adrian S. Wisnicki and Megan Ward (2004–21), <http://livingstoneonline.org/uuid/node/cobd18cf-692f-4843-b896-799cff98351b> [accessed 10 October 2023].

(c) Citing plays and longer poems

The first full reference to a play or other long, subdivided work (e.g. a poem in cantos) should indicate the edition used. Small capital roman numerals should be used for the numbers of acts of plays, and for the numbers of 'books', cantos, and other major subdivisions. Smaller subdivisions (scenes, chapters, etc.) and line numbers are usually indicated by arabic numerals. Later references and the identification of quotations should be given in the form: *Macbeth*, III. 4. 99–107, *Samson Agonistes*, I. 819. Note that figures in references should be separated by full stops (not commas) and spaces, e.g.:

> *The Merchant of Venice*, II. 3. 10
> *The Faerie Queene*, III. 8. 26
> *Paradise Lost*, IX. 342–50
> *Aeneid*, VI. 215–18
> *Gerusalemme liberata*, III. 9
> *City of God*, XIX. 2

(d) Citing the Bible

References should be in the following form:

> Isaiah 22. 17
> II Corinthians 5. 13–15

Books of the Bible are not italicized. Small capital roman numerals are used for the numbers of books before the book title. Arabic numerals, separated by a full stop and a space, are used for chapters and verses.

§7.4. Citing Journal Articles

The first reference should be given in full in a form similar to that in the following examples:

(i) Doriane Zerka, 'Constructing Poetic Identity: Iberia as a Heterotopia in Oswald von Wolkenstein's Songs', *MLR*, 114.2 (2019), pp. 274–93 (p. 279), doi:10.5699/modelangrevi.114.2.0274.

(ii) Michael Rothberg, 'Decolonizing Trauma Studies: A Response', *Studies in the Novel*, 40.1–2 (2008), pp. 224–34 (p. 227), doi:10.1353/sdn.0.0005.

(iii) Helena Taylor, 'Ancients, Moderns, Gender: Marie-Jeanne L'Héritier's "Le Parnasse reconnoissant, ou, Le triomphe de Madame Des-Houlières"', *French Studies*, 71.1 (2017), pp. 15–30, doi:10.1093/fs/knw261.

(iv) Roya Biggie, 'The Botany of Colonization in John Fletcher's *The Island Princess*', *Renaissance Drama*, 50.2 (2022), pp. 159–87 (pp. 166–67), doi:10.1086/722938.

(v) Russell West-Pavlov, 'Modernism and Modernities in Achebe's *Things Fall Apart*', *English Studies in Africa*, 65.1 (2022), pp. 72–86, doi:10.1080/00138398.2022.205586.

(vi) Eduardo Urbina, 'Don Quijote, *puer–senex*: un tópico y su transformación paródica en el *Quijote*', *Journal of Hispanic Philology*, 12 (1987–88), pp. 127–38.

(vii) Christine Acham, 'Black-ish: Kenya Barris on Representing Blackness in the Age of Black Lives Matter', *Film Quarterly*, 71.3 (2018), pp. 48–57, doi:10.1525/fq.2018.71.3.48.

(viii) Judith Pollmann, 'Of Living Legends and Authentic Tales: How to Get Remembered in Early Modern Europe', *Transactions of the Royal Historical Society*, 6th ser., 23 (2013), pp. 103–25, doi:10.1017/S0080440113000054.

(ix) Jacob Wirshba, review of Naama Harel, *Kafka's Zoopoetics: Beyond the Human-Animal Barrier* (2020), *MLR*, 117.1 (2022), pp. 140–41, doi:10.1353/mlr.2022.0032.

(x) [Anon.], review of Shane Weller, *The Idea of Europe: A Critical History* (2021), *Forum for Modern Language Studies*, 58 (2022), pp. 134–35, doi:10.1093/fmls/cqac019.

(xi) Gavriel D. Rosenfeld, 'The Rise of Illiberal Memory', *Memory Studies*, published online 15 February 2021, doi:10.1177/1750698020988771.

The information should be given in the following order:

Author's name, exactly as it appears in the article (for multiple authors see §7.3 (a)).

Title of article, in single quotation marks.

Title of journal, italicized.

An indication of the series in cases where the journal has had more than one series, e.g. 'n.s.' for 'new series'.

Volume number, in arabic numerals.

Full point and part number, in arabic numerals, if the volume has multiple parts. If two part numbers have been published together, this should be cited as in example ii. It is not necessary to give the season or month of publication, e.g. (Spring 2020).

Year(s) of publication, in parentheses. Omit parentheses if there is no volume number.

First and last page numbers of article cited, preceded by 'pp.'.

Page number(s), in parentheses and preceded by 'p.' or 'pp.', of the particular reference (if necessary).

DOI, if one is available, preceded by 'doi:'. There is no space between the colon and the number. Almost all scholarly articles now have DOIs, even if published before the digital age, but there are exceptions. With a DOI, it is not necessary to give an access date. A URL should only be given where there is no DOI. Do not give the name of the database through which you accessed the article, e.g. JSTOR or EBSCO.

The use of the colon to separate the title and subtitle in an article, the norms for capitalization within the title and subtitle, the treatment of the titles of works of literature occurring within the titles of articles, and references to particular pages within an article are, as the examples illustrate, treated in the same way as for chapters in edited collections (see §7.3 (b)).

Journals follow their own capitalization rules for the titles of articles, which can vary widely; disregard these in favour of the rules presented here, in order that your references are consistent. For example, an article printed in the journal *Science* as 'Mortality risk from United States coal electricity generation' would be cited in MHRA style as 'Mortality Risk from United States Coal Electricity Generation'.

Only the main title of a journal should be given. Any subtitle and the place of publication should be omitted unless they serve to distinguish between two journals of the same name. An initial definite or indefinite article should be omitted except when the title consists of the article and one other word, e.g. *La Linguistique*. The titles of journals should be abbreviated only when the abbreviation is likely to be more familiar to readers than the full title (e.g. *PMLA*), otherwise the title should be given in full. If the journal title is abbreviated to initials, full stops should not be used (see example i; for rules on stops in abbreviations, see §2.10). For the proceedings of learned societies, etc., the name of the organization should be italicized as part of the title (e.g. *Proceedings of the British Academy*).

The volume number should be given in arabic numerals, no matter what the style preferred by the journal (e.g. *Medium Ævum*, 58, *not* LVIII). The number should not be preceded by 'vol.'.

If the journal describes itself as covering an academic year rather than a calendar year, this should be indicated as in example vi.

An article that has been published online by a journal but not yet assigned to a volume should be cited as in example xi. Do not give the volume number as 0 or 00.0 even if the publisher or journal host presents the citation data in this format.

To cite a complete issue of a journal (for instance, a special issue on an author or topic), give the title and editors as you would for a book, followed by 'special issue of' and the journal data. For example:

> (xii) *Modern Portuguese Poetry*, ed. by Paulo de Medeiros and Rosa Maria Martelo, special issue of *Portuguese Studies*, 36.2 (2020).

§7.5. Citing Websites and Social Media

This section covers the procedures for citing websites and social media which do not have DOIs. To cite journal articles, which have DOIs, see §7.4; for general information about the role of DOIs and URLs, see §6.1; on formatting URLs, see §6.3. Follow these examples:

> (i) Amel Mukhtar, 'How Failure Freed Coco Jones, R&B's Soulful New Star', *British Vogue*, 28 March 2023 <https://www.vogue.co.uk/arts-and-lifestyle/article/coco-jones-interview> [accessed 4 April 2023].

(ii) 'Welcome to the MHRA Style Guide Online', MHRA, n.d. <https://www.mhra.org.uk/style> [accessed 1 December 2023].

(iii) LEGO Ideas, 'Hungry? 🌭', Facebook, 20 April 2023 <https://www.facebook.com/LEGOIdeas/photos/a.325471264133745/6706754659338675> [accessed 21 April 2023].

(iv) Virago Press (@ViragoBooks), '💙 Some readers have told us they always shed a tear at the ending of Carrie's War', Twitter, 10 April 2023 <https://twitter.com/ViragoBooks/status/1645445347378970624> [accessed 27 April 2023].

(v) 'What's On At Tate', Tate, n.d. <https://www.tate.org.uk/whats-on> [accessed 6 October 2023].

(vi) PurpleFerret9146, 'What do you think about Normal People by Sally Rooney?', Reddit, 17 April 2023 <https://www.reddit.com/r/literature/comments/12oyh4k/what_do_you_think_about_normal_people_by_sally> [accessed 27 April 2023].

(vii) 'The Bloody Chamber and Other Stories', goodreads, n.d. <https://www.goodreads.com/book/show/49011.The_Bloody_Chamber_and_Other_Stories> [accessed 1 January 2023].

(viii) 'Visualization', 15cBooktrade, 18 June 2016 <https://wordpress-prd.bodleian.ox.ac.uk/booktrade/wp-content/uploads/sites/4/2015/05/Visualisation-18-June-2016.png> [accessed 20 November 2023].

In general, give as much of the following information as is available and applicable:

(1) Author name, followed by username, where relevant, in parenthesis; if only a username is present, this can be given in place of the author name (with no parenthesis). Follow the capitalization employed by the user.

(2) Title of page or article, in single quotation marks. For shorter posts such as those on social media, the post itself can be given as the title; starting at the first word, cite the shortest portion that makes sense. Spelling, punctuation, capitalization, and italicization should follow that used in the original. Include emojis, #hashtags, and @usernames where present.

(3) Platform or publisher. This can be either the platform that hosts the text or the website on which the page is located. Names of services or platforms such as YouTube, Snapchat, or TikTok should be given in roman type. Names of websites are generally given in roman (e.g. British Museum, Deutscher Bundestag) but may be given in italics if the website is the equivalent of a print publication (e.g. *FiveThirtyEight*, *art21 magazine*). If a social media platform

changes its name, give the name that was current at the time the original post was made.

(4) Date. Give as much information as is present. If the page is undated, give 'n.d.'. Including the time of day (e.g. for a social media post) is not usually necessary.

(5) URL, in angle brackets (see §6.3).

(6) Date of access, in square brackets. The most recent date on which you accessed the page or post.

For entries in major reference works with a search function, give the search term and the URL of the main website only:

> (ix) Entry 'style', *Oxford English Dictionary*, n.d. <https://www.oed.com> [accessed 11 September 2023].

Comments on online material can be cited via the username of the comment author, then 'comment on', followed by the full reference to the original post as above. The date remains the date of the original post, rather than of the comment:

> (x) Topaz_hunter, comment on Jeremy Gray, 'The Winners of the GDT Nature Photographer of the Year 2023', PetaPixel, 21 April 2023 <https://petapixel.com/2023/04/21/the-winners-of-the-gdt-nature-photographer-of-the-year-2023> [accessed 27 April 2023].

§7.6. Citing Newspaper Articles

References to articles in newspapers or magazines (periodical publications other than scholarly journals organized by volume and/or part) follow the same general rules as journal articles (see §7.4), but normally require only the date of issue (day, month, and year).

> (i) Ian Thomson, 'Italo Calvino: A Celebration of the Fairy King', *Daily Telegraph*, 19 September 2015 <https://www.telegraph.co.uk/books/what-to-read/italo-calvino-the-fairy-king/> [accessed 2 February 2023].

> (ii) Olivier Ubertalli, 'Entre Antoine Gallimard et Vincent Bolloré, la guerre du livre', *Le Point*, 25 February 2023 <https://www.lepoint.fr/medias/entre-antoine-gallimard-et-vincent-bollore-la-guerre-du-livre-25-02-2023-2509972_260.php> [accessed 6 March 2023].

(iii) Hannah Clugston, '"If Not Now, When?" Review: A Timely Tour through Feminist Sculpture', *Guardian*, 3 April 2023 <https://www.theguardian.com/artanddesign/2023/apr/03/if-not-now-when-review-wakefield-post-hepworth-survey-female-narrative-sculpture> [accessed 3 April 2023].

(iv) Egbert Tholl, 'Schauspielhaus Zürich. Beim Geld hört die Wokeness auf', *Süddeutsche Zeitung*, 6 March 2023 <https://www.sueddeutsche.de/kultur/gier-zuercher-schspielhaus-christopher-rueping-intendanz-1.5763717> [accessed 17 June 2023].

Initial '*The*' or '*A*' is normally omitted when citing English-language newspapers and magazines, with the exception of *The Times*.

The date of issue (with the month always in English) should be given between commas, *not* parentheses.

Page numbers are normally only necessary for older or archival material.

When citing articles in literary magazines, treat them as you would journal articles (with 'p.' or 'pp.' before the page number(s)), but use the system used by the magazine itself for identifying issues.

(v) Fatima Bhutto, 'The Hour of the Wolf', *Granta*, 158 (2022), pp. 9–25.

(vi) José Luis Pardo, 'Filosofía y clausura de la modernidad', *Revista de Occidente*, 66 (1986), pp. 35–47.

(vii) E. Iukina, 'Dostoinstvo cheloveka', *Novyi mir*, 1984, no. 12, pp. 245–48.

§7.7. Citing Manuscripts

Names of manuscript repositories and collections should be given in full in the first instance and an abbreviated form should be used for subsequent references. The degree of abbreviation which may be acceptable will depend upon the frequency with which a particular repository, collection, or manuscript is referred to and upon any possible ambiguities. The names of manuscript collections should be given in roman type without quotation marks and the citation of manuscripts within collections should be according to the system of classification of the repository.

The following examples show a suggested method of citation for first references and possible models for later references. Note that, because of the danger of ambiguity, 'fol.' and 'fols' are preferred to 'f.' and 'ff.'. The abbreviated and superscript forms for 'recto' and 'verso' are also preferred:

fol. 3^r, fol. 127^v, fols 17^v–22^r, fols 17^{r-v}

First reference	Later references
London, British Library, Cotton MS Caligula D III, fol. 15^r	Cotton MS Caligula D III, fols 17^v–19^r
Oxford, Bodleian Library, MS Bodley 277	MS Bodley 277
Sheffield Central Library (CL), MS Fitzwilliam E.209	Sheffield CL, MS Fitzwilliam E.209
Paris, Bibliothèque nationale de France (BnF), MS fonds français 1124	BnF, MS f. fr. 1124
Florence, Biblioteca Riccardiana (BRF), MS 2306	BRF, MS 2306, fol. 10^r
Paris, Archives nationales de France (AN), H.486 bis. 172	AN, H.486 bis. 172

§7.8. Citing Music, Film, Television, and Software

References to specific recordings of music or speech should incorporate the following items, as applicable: composer, author, or performing artist; title of song, in roman and single quotation marks; title of piece, compilation, album, etc., in italics (preceded by 'from' if an individual song or section is being cited as well); orchestra, conductor, etc., separated by commas; recording company and date in parentheses.

> (i) Ludwig van Beethoven, *Piano Concerto no. 5*, Mitsuko Uchida, Symphonieorchester des Bayerischen Rundfunks, cond. by Kurt Sanderling (Phillips, 1998).
>
> (ii) Dylan Thomas, *Under Milk Wood*, read by Anthony Hopkins and Jonathan Pryce (Listening for Pleasure, 1992).
>
> (iii) The Beatles, *Penny Lane/Strawberry Fields Forever* (EMI, 1967).
>
> (iv) Black Sabbath, 'Into the Void', from *Master of Reality* (Vertigo, 1971).
>
> (v) Kate Bush, 'Strange Phenomena', from *The Kick Inside* (EMI, 1978).
>
> (vi) John Cale, 'Hallelujah', from *Fragments of a Rainy Season* (Hannibal Records, 1992).

With modern music which originates as recordings by an artist or group, give the artist name first, then the title of the track in single quotes, and then details of the album on which it was first released, as in examples iv–vi. In the case of a single not drawn from an album, give the title of the single, as in iii. It is not normally useful to cite the song's composer, since commercial music services are searchable primarily by the song or artist name, not by the songwriter's. In example vi, Cale's cover version of Leonard Cohen's much-covered standard 'Hallelujah' thus appears under Cale's name, not Cohen's. If relevant, the original composer/songwriter may be given after the song title, as in the following example:

>   (vii) Sinéad O'Connor, 'Nothing Compares 2 U', by Prince, from *I Do Not Want What I Haven't Got* (Chrysalis Records, 1990).

For films, the reference should include, as a minimum, title, director, country, and date. If relevant to your discussion, you may add information such as details of a subsequent release or extra material on a DVD. For example:

>   (viii) *The Grapes of Wrath*, dir. by John Ford (USA, 1940).
>
>   (ix) *Der geteilte Himmel*, dir. by Konrad Wolf (East Germany, 1964).
>
>   (x) *Blade Runner*, dir. by Ridley Scott (USA, 1982; Director's Cut, 1992).

Only cite a DVD or Blu-Ray release if you are quoting from material specific to that release, e.g. a director's commentary.

>   (xi) *Hermann, mein Vater*, dir. by Helma Sanders-Brahms (West Germany, 1987), documentary included on the Blu-Ray release of *Deutschland, bleiche Mutter*, dir. by Helma Sanders-Brahms (West Germany, 1980; BFI, 2015).

For television series and programmes, cite as follows:

>   (xii) *Battlestar Galactica*, David Eick Productions (British Sky Broadcasting, 2004–09).
>
>   (xiii) 'Guy Walks into an Advertising Agency', *Mad Men* (Lionsgate Television, 2007–15), season 3, episode 6 (2009).

Give the date of a broadcast only if this is relevant, which might be the case with a current affairs or news programme, or a historically significant broadcast. For example:

>   (xiv) Brian Hanrahan, 'East Germany Opens the Gates', *BBC News*, BBC 1, 9 November 1989.
>
>   (xv) *Newsnight*, BBC 2, 24 February 2022.

For music and video on general release, do not cite the website of the streaming service you used to access it.

References to software should provide the author or designer (if identifiable), the title in italics, the studio (if other than the author), the date, and the platform, e.g.:

>   (xvi) Emily Short, *Galatea* (2000), Z-machine.
>
>   (xvii) Id Software, *Doom* (1993), MS-DOS and subsequently other platforms.
>
>   (xviii) Stuart Gillespie-Cook and others, *Untitled Goose Game* (House House, 2019), macOS, Windows, Switch, PlayStation 4, and Xbox One.

§7.9. Citing Works of Art

References to works of art should include at least the name of the artist (if known), the title of the work in italics (see §3.8), its date (if known), and the medium of composition. Titles should normally be given in their most customary English-language form, where there is one. Depending on the medium, the dimensions (in cm) and a current physical location or source may also be given. When giving dimensions, note the use of a multiplication sign, not a lower case 'x', and the spaces around it. For example:

>   (i) Piero della Francesca, *The Flagellation*, c. 1455, oil and tempera on panel, 59 × 82 cm, Galleria Nazionale delle Marche, Urbino.
>
>   (ii) Cornelia Parker, *Island*, 2022, mixed media, Tate Britain.
>
>   (iii) Ansel Adams, *Monolith, the Face of Half Dome*, 1927, silver gelatin print, 14.6 × 19.7 cm.
>
>   (iv) Alphonse Mucha, *Bières de la Meuse*, 1897, colour lithograph, 154.5 × 104.5 cm.

See §1.3 (b) for the wording of captions to illustrations, which follow a different format.

Reference an exhibition catalogue as you would any other book, e.g.:

>   (v) Luke Syson, with Larry Keith and others, *Leonardo da Vinci: Painter at the Court of Milan* (National Gallery Company, 2011).

§7.10. Citing Theses and Other Unpublished Scholarship

The titles of unpublished theses and dissertations should be in roman type within single quotation marks; capitalization should follow the conventions of the language in question (see §3.4). The degree level (where known), university, and date should be in parentheses. A URL should be given if available:

> (i) Qian Shen, 'Hombres en un mundo de mujeres: estereotipos e identidades masculinas en el cine de Pedro Almodóvar' (unpublished doctoral thesis, Universidad Complutense de Madrid, 2018) <https://eprints.ucm.es/id/eprint/50725/> [accessed 10 November 2023].
>
> (ii) Philip Sulter, 'Beyond the Post-9/11 Novel: Representations of State Violence and Imperialism in Fictions of the War on Terror' (unpublished doctoral thesis, University of Manchester, 2021), pp. 145–68 <https://research.manchester.ac.uk/en/studentTheses/beyond-the-post-911-novel-representations-of-state-violence-and-i> [accessed 1 June 2023].
>
> (iii) Nil Melissa Von Baibus, 'In Pursuit of Collective Laughter: Bergson, Bakhtin, and Contemporary Conceptions of the Comic' (unpublished master's thesis, University of Bristol, 2022), p. 238 <https://research-information.bris.ac.uk/en/studentTheses/in-pursuit-of-collective-laughter> [accessed 5 October 2023].

American universities distinguish between a master's 'thesis' and a doctoral 'dissertation':

> (iv) Corley E. Humphrey, '"You Never Get it Out of Your Bones": The Christ-Haunted Security of Jean Louise "Scout" Finch in Harper Lee's *To Kill a Mockingbird* and *Go Set a Watchman*' (unpublished master's thesis, Liberty University, 2021), pp. 43–51 <https://digitalcommons.liberty.edu/masters/723/> [accessed 15 June 2023].
>
> (v) John Park, 'Prosaic Times: Time as Subject in Wordsworth, Richardson, Flaubert, and Melville' (unpublished doctoral dissertation, Princeton University, 2020), p. 289 <https://dataspace.princeton.edu/handle/88435/dsp018910jx63h> [accessed 2 January 2023].

Generally, it is preferable to cite scholarship that has been peer-reviewed and published. Scholarship available in open-access preprint repositories may be cited using the conventions for citing online material. If citing a conference paper that you have attended, endeavour to find or secure a written copy. This can then be cited as for online material (see §7.5) or personal correspondence (see §7.11). If it is not possible to secure a written copy, the material can be cited as follows:

> (vi) Derek Connon, 'A Two-Headed Eagle: Cocteau's Play and Film', unpublished paper delivered at the conference 'Adaptation: Intertextual Transformations across Different Media' (Swansea University, July 2015).

§7.11. Citing Interviews and Correspondence

An interview previously published can be cited as normal, for instance as a journal article, newspaper article, or online video. Follow the source in assigning authorship to the interviewer, the interviewee, or both. If it is unclear, treat the interviewer as the author. If the title of the interview does not make clear who is being interviewed, add 'interview with X' after the title. For example:

>   (i) Robbie Collin, 'The Future of Cinema: An Interview with Sir Steve McQueen CBE', *The Telegraph*, 23 April 2021 <https://www.youtube.com/watch?v=OLEFx6a47Zk> [27 June 2023].
>
>   (ii) Jenise Hudson and Janeen Price, 'Interview with Claudia Rankine', *CLA Journal*, 60.1 (2016), pp. 10–14.
>
>   (iii) Julian Petley, Danièle Huillet, and Jean-Marie Straub, 'Interview with Danièle Huillet and Jean-Marie Straub apropos *The Death of Empedocles* and *Black Sin*, 9 April 1990, Goethe-Institut London', in *The Cinema of Danièle Huillet and Jean-Marie Straub*, ed. by Martin Brady and Helen Hughes (Legenda, 2023), pp. 196–209.
>
>   (iv) Deborah Solomon, 'A Gloom of Her Own', interview with Elfriede Jelinek, *New York Times*, 21 November 2004 <https://www.nytimes.com/2004/11/21/magazine/a-gloom-of-her-own.html> [accessed 27 June 2023].

In the case of a published letter, give the writer as the author and if possible the addressee. For example:

>   (v) Philip Larkin, letter to C. Day Lewis, 22 September 1971, in *Selected Letters of Philip Larkin 1940–1985*, ed. by Anthony Thwaite (Faber, 1992), pp. 446–47.
>
>   (vi) Jacques Henri Bernardin de Saint-Pierre, letter to Joseph Jérôme Lefrançois de Lalande, 23 February 1791, ed. by Malcolm Cook (2013), in *Digital Correspondence of Bernardin de Saint-Pierre*, ed. by Malcolm Cook and others (Electronic Enlightenment, 2008–22), doi:10.13051/ee:mss/sainjaVF0030816a1c.
>
>   (vii) Elizabeth Montagu, letter to James Beattie, 4 July 1791, ed. by Caroline Franklin, Michael Franklin, and Nicole Pohl, in *Elizabeth Montagu Correspondence Online*, ed. by Nicole Pohl and others <https://emco.swansea.ac.uk/emco/letter-view/1900/> [accessed 10 October 2023].

If you have access to unpublished interviews or correspondence (for example, if an author has written to you directly or you have recorded a conversation with a director or artist), cite it as follows:

> Derek Walcott, email to the author, 23 March 2012.
> Maggie O'Farrell, interview with the author, 14 November 2020.
> Alison Bechdel, letter to the author, 20 August 2021.

Note that copyright in a letter or email resides with the writer, even if the letter was written to you, so that you cannot reproduce it in print without the permission of the author. The same normally applies to interviews, conversations, etc., even if you were personally involved.

§7.12. Abbreviated References to Works Already Cited

In all references to the same source after the first, the shortest unambiguous form should be used. A shortened reference signals that a full reference has already been given and your reader must be able to match the shortened form to the earlier full form.

In a monograph or thesis, treat each chapter independently for this purpose. That is, give a full reference for a source at its first mention in the chapter, and shortened references later in that chapter. If it occurs again in a later chapter, give the full reference again at its first mention there.

The abbreviated reference will normally be the author's name followed by the title (abbreviated where appropriate, for example by dropping any subtitle), volume number (if applicable), and page reference:

> Kokobobo and McFadden, 'The Queer Nihilist', p. 125.
> Pimentel, *From Arcadia to Revolution*, p. 56.
> Ireton, 'Adalbert Stifter', p. 220.
> Wirshba, review of Naama Harel, p. 140.
> Zerka, 'Constructing Poetic Identity', p. 279.

Sometimes, particularly in the case of editions of an author's works or collections of essays, a short-title form of reference may be more appropriate:

> *Simone de Beauvoir: Mémoires*, II, p. 35.
> *Chaucer, Langland, Arthur*, pp. 212–44 (p. 229).
> *Homeri Ilias*, II, pp. 78–79.

Where you have already cited in full a collected volume of essays and now wish to cite a second essay from the same volume, you may shorten the title and editors' names, and omit the publication details of the volume:

Sabine Nöllgen, 'The Darkness of the Anthropocene: Wolfgang Hilbig's *Alte Abdeckerei*', in *Readings in the Anthropocene*, ed. by Wilke and Johnstone, pp. 148–66.

A second reference to the same essay would then appear as:

Nöllgen, 'The Darkness of the Anthropocene', p. 155.

The expressions 'loc. cit.' and 'op. cit.' are too vague and should not be used. The term 'ibid.' should be used very sparingly and limited to those situations where there is no possibility of confusion, such as after a second reference which is separated from its predecessor by no more than four lines of typescript. Do not use 'ibid.' to abbreviate only part of a reference: use 'Ibid., pp. 45–71' not 'Jones, ibid., pp. 45–71'. Use the capitalized form 'Ibid.' at the start of a note. Do not use 'id.' or 'eadem'.

For repeated references to medieval manuscripts, a more formal system of abbreviations can be used: see §7.7.

§7.13. The Author–Date System

The author–date system uses short in-text references that can be readily matched to a corresponding bibliography item containing the publication details in full. The bibliographical references are placed at the end of the book, article, or thesis.

References in the text should give, in parentheses, the surname(s) of the author(s) (adding initials if needed to distinguish authors with the same surname), the publication date of the work, and, where necessary, a page reference, which should be preceded by a colon. If two or more works by the same author have the same publication date they should be distinguished by adding letters after the dates ('2017a', '2017b', etc.). For example:

While the word 'disability' was certainly part of a Romantic-era vocabulary, its use in that period does not match its use today, which means that care must be taken when applying the word retrospectively (Joshua 2020: 1–2).

There is ample evidence that 'early moderns relied on human–plant similarities to think through the perceived risks and benefits of transplantation' (Biggie 2022: 174).

Recent studies of literary motherhood (notably Rye and others 2017) stress the role played by literary texts in exploring maternal ambivalence.

Rosi Braidotti's thinking on posthumanism has been widely applied to literary texts, for instance to Bowen's 'The Demon Lover' (P. Mukherjee 2021).

Áine O'Healy identifies a new wave of Italian film in which 'immigration is envisioned neither as a novelty nor a pressing emergency but rather as part of everyday urban life' (2019a: 178).

When the author's name is given in the text, it need not be repeated in a reference given in the same sentence: e.g., do not write 'Smith (Smith 2021) argues that...'. In such cases, the reference either follows the name or, if this seems stylistically preferable, may come at some other point in the same sentence:

Smith (2022: 66) argues that [...]

Smith, who was known for his contentious views, replied (2022: 75) that [...]

Smith regards this interpretation as 'wholly unacceptable' (2022: 81).

The bibliography in a book takes slightly different forms according to whether the citation with notes system or the author–date system has been used in the main text: see §8.3 and §8.4 respectively.

8 • Bibliographies and Indexes

This chapter covers the way in which the information in a bibliography or index is to be set out. The first two sections apply to both bibliographies and indexes; they cover the ordering of names and terms alphabetically. This is followed by information about how to set out a bibliography or list of works cited in each of the two key referencing systems — citation in notes and author-date citation. Finally, advice is given on what to include in an index and how to organize index entries so that readers can easily find the information they require.

§8.1. Inverting Names in Indexes and Bibliographies

A name must first be put into the right format for indexing or listing. For many Western names, this is very straightforward: simply invert the surname and forename and separate them with a comma.

McEwan, Ian
Ransmayr, Christoph
Vendler, Helen

In general, there is no need to give middle names unless authors always publish using a middle name or initial, such as:

Alcott, Louisa May
Jerome, Jerome K.
Proulx, E. Annie

Middle names, where needed, should be placed last, but compound surnames are more difficult, because they depend on the preferences or fame of the subject. For example, we would write Clinton, Hillary Rodham, not Rodham Clinton, Hillary, because she is almost always associated with her married name and not her birth name; but the critic of Spanish colonial literature in the New World should be inverted as Castellví Laukamp, Luis, not as Laukamp, Luis Castellví. While it is more common for Hispanic compound surnames to be treated in this way, each case in practice comes down to the preferences of the owner of the name.

Patronymics and similar particles, like the French honorific 'de', sometimes appear before and sometimes after the surname. As a general rule, if they are normally capitalized (as is the case with Ní Dhúill) then they come first, and if not then second. A historical figure such as Charles de Gaulle, who is always designated as 'de Gaulle' in contemporary accounts, would be an exception. Thus:

> Ní Dhúill, Caitríona
> Neumann, John von
> Balzac, Honoré de
> Orléans, Adélaïde d'
> de Gaulle, Charles

Welsh names containing *ap* or *ab* are another exception. Names of historical figures are not inverted at all, while more recent names invert to begin with the *ap* or *ab*:

> Maredudd ab Owain
> ap Gwilym, Myrddin

Spelling and capitalization can be variable for French authors before the modern age. The library catalogue of the Bibliothèque nationale de France, <https://catalogue.bnf.fr> [accessed 10 May 2023], may be helpful as an arbiter.

Pseudonyms and common-use names which differ from 'real' names also present an issue. A bibliography entry citing a pseudonymous work should certainly use the pseudonym, since that is what is printed as the author name, but an index might want to include the real name too. Some cultural figures come to be known under familiar names over time, such as Byron, or Donatello; and some contemporary figures have customary names already, such as Lula, the present President of Brazil. In such cases, good indexing style is to place the more familiar name first, and then give the proper names in brackets, where it is useful to do so.

> Byron (George Gordon, Lord Byron)
> Carlos the Jackal (Ilich Ramírez Sánchez)
> Chanel, Coco (Gabrielle Chanel)
> Ford Madox Ford (Joseph Madox Hueffer)
> Lula (Luiz Inácio Lula da Silva)

There is no need to be overly pedantic: an index or bibliography is meant to serve the book which contains it, and not to be a reference work to full names of cultural figures.

Where an author or artist has produced work before and after changing their name (for instance through marriage or gender transition, or to reflect their heritage), and where it is necessary to include both names, give their current name followed by the previous name in brackets:

Tempest, Kae (formerly Kate)
Newton, Thandiwe (formerly Thandie)
Wachowski, Lana (formerly Laurence)

As noted in §8.2 below, if readers are likely to look up such a name under more than one form, use cross-reference entries so that each form is covered. For example:

Alighieri, Dante, *see* Dante

Where titles are given, they should appear after a name, divided by a comma:

Alfonso X, King of Castile
Anselm of Canterbury, St
Humphrey, Duke of Gloucester

With regnal names, it is sensible to give the country if the book being indexed involves monarchs of more than one nation: John, King of England, is a different person from John, King of Bohemia. But if indexing a book which discusses only England, this is unlikely to be necessary.

§8.2. Sorting in Alphabetical Order

There are two common forms of alphabetization in use today, which differ only in how they handle multi-word entries: word alphabetization, sorting by each word in turn, and letter alphabetization, in which the spacing between words is ignored. To see the difference, consider:

German thought
Germanic literature

In word alphabetization, German comes before Germanic, and so 'German thought' comes before 'Germanic literature'; in letter alphabetization, they are the other way around, because 'germanicliterature' precedes 'germanthought' at the seventh letter.

MHRA style is to use word alphabetization for indexes and bibliographies, as is traditional in the publishing industry. Be warned, however, that word processors sometimes use letter alphabetization when sorting by default, because that is more usual for electronic catalogues and dictionaries.

Sort using the English alphabet. Treat accented letters as if they have no accent:

Süßmann, Christel
Sußmann, Hans

However, if two entries are identical in all respects other than an accent, place the unaccented version first:
> Hebert, Ernest
> Hébert, Ernest
> Munster
> Münster

In a book on Welsh studies, it may be sensible to follow Welsh orthography and sort digraphs such as LL as if they were single letters, but in a list which contains only one or two Welsh names, this is more likely to confuse than assist a reader. In Scandinavian languages, Æ, Ø, and Å sort after Z, and in that order. And in all languages, numbers should come before A: thus '99 Luftballons' comes before 'Allein Allein'.

If a reader may look up a name under more than one form, use a cross-reference. For example:
> Alighieri, Dante, *see* Dante
> de Beauvoir, Simone, *see* Beauvoir, Simone de

As noted below, within a given author's entry in a bibliography, it may be necessary to alphabetize works by title, and the same can apply to index subentries:
> Dickens, Charles:
> > *The Cricket on the Hearth: A Fairy Tale of Home*
> > *Hard Times*
> > *The Pickwick Papers*
> > *A Tale of Two Cities*

In general, the rules for alphabetizing titles are the same as for names: again, use word alphabetization. However, note that in English, the articles 'A', 'An', and 'The' should be ignored if they occur as the first word in a title. Thus *An Unquiet Mind* is alphabetized as if it were simply *Unquiet Mind*.

In other languages conventions may vary. In French, it is customary to ignore definite articles, but not indefinite articles. Thus *Le Cabinet du docteur Caligari* appears under C, but *Une famille formidable* under U.

§8.3. Bibliography with Citation in Notes

Where you have used footnotes or endnotes to reference sources, you may be asked to supply an alphabetical bibliography or list of works cited. If you are writing a book this will almost always be needed; some, but not all, journals also ask for a bibliography.

Web pages and the like can normally be included alphabetically among books, chapters, and journal articles in the normal way. However, some sources such as films, medieval manuscripts, or extensive online databases do not so easily belong to a regular bibliography. It may then be sensible to divide those categories off into a separate section of entries, such as a filmography, or a list of manuscripts and the libraries holding them.

In nearly all respects, the material provided in a bibliography matches that provided in notes, in terms of both information and presentation. The main exception to this is the treatment of names.

The name of the author or editor of a work is reversed, as detailed in §8.1 above, with the surname preceding the forename, middle name, and/or any initials. Where a work has multiple authors, this applies only to the first author: do not reverse the normal order of names after the first.

If a work has more than three authors, list only the first, followed by 'and others'. Do not use 'et al.'.

For an edited collection of contributed chapters, the editor's name comes first, inverted as above, followed by 'ed.' or 'eds' as appropriate, placed within brackets.

For editions of an author's work, the work should normally be listed under the author's name, and the name(s) of the editor/translator should follow the title, preceded by 'ed. by' or 'trans. by', as is the practice in notes. In some cases (such as a large collected works of a classic author), the author's name might form part of the title; in such cases, it may be preferable to list the work under the editor's name.

Anonymous works, television series, or other works where there is no obvious author, such as a website, are listed under their title, ignoring any initial definite or indefinite article when determining alphabetical order.

If two or more essays in the same edited volume are cited, the bibliography should have separate entries for each essay, rather than one entry for the volume as a whole. Give the full details of the volume for each separate bibliography entry. This does not exclude also listing the volume separately under its editor(s) if it is felt to be a valuable resource. In general, it is sensible to avoid cross-references within a bibliography.

Unlike in a note, there is no full stop at the end of a bibliography entry.

In all other respects, the information in a bibliography entry matches the information in the corresponding note and authors should check this carefully. Whichever name has been used for short forms of reference in the notes (see §7.12) will be the name readers look up in the bibliography. The following examples illustrate these points:

> *Battlestar Galactica*, David Eick Productions (British Sky Broadcasting, 2004–09)
>
> *La Chanson de Roland* (Grasset, 1990)
>
> Fonseca Pimentel, Eleonora, *From Arcadia to Revolution: 'The Neapolitan Monitor' and Other Writings*, ed. and trans. by Verina R. Jones (Iter Press and Arizona Center for Medieval and Renaissance Studies, 2019)
>
> Jeannelle, Jean-Louis, and others (eds), *Simone de Beauvoir: Mémoires*, 2 vols (Gallimard, 2018)
>
> Kokobobo, Ani, 'Tolstoy's Enigmatic Final Hero: War, Sufism, and the Spiritual Path in *Hadji Murat*', *Russian Review*, 76.1 (2017), pp. 38–52, doi:10.1111/russ.12118
>
> Kokobobo, Ani, and Devin McFadden, 'The Queer Nihilist: Queer Time, Social Refusal, and Heteronormativity in *The Precipice*', in *Goncharov in the Twenty-First Century*, ed. by Ingrid Kleespies and Lyudmila Parts (Academic Studies Press, 2021), pp. 132–52, doi:10.2307/j.ctv249sgs4.13
>
> Rothberg, Michael, 'Decolonizing Trauma Studies: A Response', *Studies in the Novel*, 40.1–2 (2008), pp. 224–34, doi:10.1353/sdn.0.0005
>
> Rye, Gill, and others (eds), *Motherhood in Literature and Culture: Interdisciplinary Perspectives from Europe* (Routledge, 2017)
>
> Shen, Qian, 'Hombres en un mundo de mujeres: estereotipos e identidades masculinas en el cine de Pedro Almodóvar' (unpublished doctoral thesis, Universidad Complutense de Madrid, 2018) <https://eprints.ucm.es/id/eprint/50725/> [accessed 10 November 2023]
>
> Taylor, Helena, 'Ancients, Moderns, Gender: Marie-Jeanne L'Héritier's "Le Parnasse reconnoissant, ou, Le triomphe de Madame Des-Houlières"', *French Studies*, 71.1 (2017), pp. 15–30, doi:10.1093/fs./knw261
>
> —— 'Antoinette Deshoulières's Cat: Polemical Equivocation in Salon Verse', *Romanic Review*, 112.3 (2021), pp. 452–69, doi:10.1215/00358118-9377358

Zava, Giulia, 'Translating the *Canzoniere* into Images: The Petrarca Queriniano Incunable', in *Translating Petrarch's Poetry: 'L'Aura del Petrarca' from the Quattrocento to the 21st Century*, ed. by Carole Birkan-Berz, Guillaume Coatelen, and Thomas Vuong (Legenda, 2020), pp. 82–102, doi:10.2307/j.ctv16kkxw0.10

In the bibliography for a book, many author entries will have multiple works. For example, the following might be the entry for the author K. F. Hilliard:

> Hilliard, K. F., 'Atemübungen: Geist und Körper in der Lyrik des 18. Jahrhunderts', in *Body Dialectics in the Age of Goethe*, ed. by Marianne Henn and Holger A. Pausch (Rodopi, 2013), pp. 293–313, doi:10.1163/9789004334359
>
> —— *Freethinkers, Libertines and Schwärmer: Heterodoxy in German Literature, 1750–1800* (Institute of Germanic and Romance Studies, 2011)
>
> —— 'Goethe and the Cure for Melancholy: "Mahomets Gesang", Orientalism and the Medical Psychology of the 18th Century', *Oxford German Studies*, 23 (1994), pp. 71–103
>
> ——, Carolin Duttlinger, and Charlie Louth (eds), *From the Enlightenment to Modernism: Three Centuries of German Literature* (Legenda, 2021)

Here a 2-em rule (typed as two consecutive em-dashes) '——' is customarily used as a form of ditto-mark, meaning that the author is the same. Works by the author alone should appear first, and then those with co-authors, if any, whose names appear after a comma.

Otherwise, works should be in alphabetical order by title, disregarding initial definite or indefinite articles. If there is an academic justification for chronological order, be sure to be consistent throughout the bibliography. For example: 'Atemübungen...', *Freethinkers*..., 'Goethe...' as solo works, and then *From*... as the only co-authored work.

Corresponding examples for a bibliography in a work that uses author–date citation (where alphabetical order is a second-order issue) are given in §8.4.

If an author or artist has produced work under more than one name (for instance following marriage, gender transition, or a name change that acknowledges their heritage), each work should be listed in the bibliography under the name under which it was published. If you are citing work under both names, it may be helpful also to provide their new or former name to enable readers to match up the names. For example:

Tempest, Kae [formerly Kate], *On Connection* (Faber, 2020)

Tempest, Kate [now Kae], *Brand New Ancients* (Picador, 2013)

The same applies where you are citing work by the same author published under multiple names. For example:

Caeiro, Alberto [heteronym of Fernando Pessoa], …

Pessoa, Fernando [*see also* Alberto Caeiro], …

§8.4. Bibliography with Author–Date Citation

A bibliography for author–date citations is presented as in the section on Bibliography with Citation in Notes above, except that the date follows the name of the author(s) or editor(s), with a full stop either side of the date:

Jeannelle, Jean-Louis, and others (eds). 2018. *Simone de Beauvoir: Mémoires*, 2 vols (Gallimard)

Joshua, Essaka. 2020. *Physical Disability in British Romantic Literature* (Cambridge University Press)

Mukherjee, Ankhi. 2010. '"What is a Classic?": International Literary Criticism and the Classic Question', *PMLA*, 125.4, pp. 1026–42

Mukherjee, Paromita. 2021. 'The Non-Human, Haunting, and the Question of "Excess" in Elizabeth Bowen's "The Demon Lover"', *Sanglap*, 8.1, pp. 41–59, doi:10.35684/JLCI.2021.8103

Tholl, Egbert. 2023. 'Schauspielhaus Zürich: Beim Geld hört die Wokeness auf', *Süddeutsche Zeitung*, 6 March <https://www.sueddeutsche.de/kultur/gier-zuercher-schspielhaus-christopher-rueping-intendanz-1.5763717> [accessed 17 June 2023]

West-Pavlov, Russell. 2022. 'Modernism and Modernities in Achebe's *Things Fall Apart*', *English Studies in Africa*, 65.1, pp. 72–86, doi:10.1080/00138398.2022.205586

As explained in §7.13, where multiple authors cited in the text share a surname, the initial letter of an author's first name is used in in-text citations as a succinct way of identifying them, e.g. '(A. Mukherjee 2010: 1035)'. In a bibliography, however, given names are written out in full, except in cases where the author has published under their initials.

If the list includes more than one work by the same author, a 2-em dash should be substituted for the name after the first appearance and works should be listed in date order. Co-authored works follow single-authored works. For example:

Hilliard, K. F. 1994. 'Goethe and the Cure for Melancholy: "Mahomets Gesang", Orientalism and the Medical Psychology of the 18th Century', *Oxford German Studies*, 23, pp. 71–103

—— 2003. 'Atemübungen: Geist und Körper in der Lyrik des 18. Jahrhunderts', in *Body Dialectics in the Age of Goethe*, ed. by Marianne Henn and Holger A. Pausch (Rodopi), pp. 293–313

—— 2011. *Freethinkers, Libertines and Schwärmer: Heterodoxy in German Literature, 1750–1800* (Institute of Germanic and Romance Studies)

——, Carolin Duttlinger, and Charlie Louth (eds). 2021. *From the Enlightenment to Modernism: Three Centuries of German Literature* (Legenda)

If two or more works by the same author(s) have the same publication date, they are arranged in alphabetical order of title and distinguished by adding letters after the date (e.g. '2019a', '2019b'):

O'Healy, Áine. 2019a. *Migrant Anxieties: Italian Cinema in a Transnational Frame* (Indiana University Press)

—— 2019b. 'Witnessing Mediterranean Migration through a Postcolonial Lens', *Imago*, 19.1, pp. 105–20

§8.5. What to Index

Most scholarly indexes should include subject-matter as well as names. It is much easier to compile a name index, but the reader of a book on America in the 1960s who needs to know about mixed marriages or monetary policy, and who finds nothing between 'Miller, Arthur' and 'Monroe, Marilyn', will feel cheated.

Names of authors and critics whose work is engaged with substantively should always be indexed. Simply quoting from a scholar probably does not warrant their inclusion in the index. Similarly, if a note simply cites a source, perhaps to justify a remark made in the text ('Baudelaire had a difficult family.'[10]), then the author of that source would not normally go into the index. Index entries should relate only to material in the body of the book; no references should be made to the bibliography pages. Index literary works under their authors (e.g.: 'Eliot, T. S., *The Sacred Wood*') unless they are anonymous, or (as in the case of some medieval texts) much better known under their titles.

If you use indexing software, be aware that it may not be able to recognize names reliably. It is also unlikely to be able to distinguish between trivial and significant keywords or to understand more complex themes and concepts, and the relationships between them. Leave time to check it by hand.

As with all authorship, the creation of an index requires human judgement rather than the following of rigid rules. Where the guidelines below would lead to unhelpful index entries, use your discretion. Keep in mind the most important aspect of an index, which is that a reader should be able to find the information they are looking for.

§8.6. Organizing an Index

For most types of work (e.g. biographies or critical studies) a single index is normally best. For others (e.g. catalogues of manuscript collections) several indexes may be needed, but keep these to a minimum.

Headings with a substantial number of page references should be subdivided: no one wants to look at all thirty-seven pages on which a person is mentioned in order to find the one that gives the date of birth. However, avoid an elaborate system of sub-entries: for many books a single level of sub-entry is sufficient.

A general rule is to use sub-entries when a main entry has more than six page references, though they may be helpful even in shorter entries.

An exception to the 'single level of sub-entries' rule may be made in the case of a book dealing with a single author, which covers a range of their works and various aspects of their life. Taking Charles Baudelaire as an example, under the index entry for his name, there may be a sub-entry 'Poems' and sub-subentries listing the poems cited in the book, in alphabetical order of title, as in this abbreviated illustration:

    Archimbaud-Dufaÿs, Caroline 2, 11
    Baudelaire, Charles:
        life:
            circumstances of birth 2
            death 231
            family 1–5
            father, *see* Baudelaire, Joseph-François
            mother, *see* Archimbaud-Dufaÿs, Caroline
        poems:
            'Abel et Caïn' 30
            'L'Albatros' 21
    Baudelaire, Joseph-François 2, 23 n. 2

It is helpful to index concepts and broad topics, but also helpful to group these as sub-entries under main entries which a reader might plausibly look up. For instance, the main entry 'censorship' might have 'of television' and 'of theatre' as sub-entries.

Apparently identical words that have different senses, or represent different parts of speech, must not be grouped in a single entry.

Substantial treatment of a topic throughout several consecutive pages is shown as e.g. '28–32'. However, passing references to that topic on each of several consecutive pages is shown as e.g. '28, 29, 30, 31, 32'.

Sub-entries should be indicated on the page by indentation. In the electronic copy, use a single tab character to achieve this rather than a series of spaces.

In general, avoid several levels of indentation, since this would lead to very short lines in a two-column index.

'See' and 'see also' should be used sparingly: cross-references are best kept to cases that are genuinely helpful. For entries referring to the same topic that have only a few page references, it is more helpful to repeat the page references, rather than supplying a cross-reference.

Entries should be placed in alphabetical order, ignoring accents or other diacritics, following the rules outlined in §8.2. Alphabetization should be checked multiple times before submission as mistakes are easily made.

Within an entry, any sub-entries must also be in alphabetical order, but an initial preposition does not count. In the following example, 'in legal documents' is deemed to begin with 'L', and so follows 'Justice':

Accademia della Crusca 13, 33, 37
Albinus, *De arte rhet. dial.* 58 n. 11
allegory 2, 15, 67–69, 101–23
    Justice 88
    in legal documents 96

§8.7. Index Entries

The following elements of indexing style are used in the MHRA's own publications. Since each publisher has its own indexing style, authors submitting work to other publishers should enquire about the publisher's preferences before beginning to compile an index.

Entries should begin with lower-case letters (except proper names or words capitalized in the text). They should end without punctuation.

No comma is necessary between the entry and the first page number, although a colon should be inserted if entries end in a numeral (for instance, '*Catch-22*: 13, 45').

A colon also appears at the end of an entry or sub-entry if there are no page numbers to the entry itself. For instance, 'Empson, William:' has a colon in the example below because there are no general page references concerning him: all of the references are in sub-entries.

For cross-referencing, follow these examples:

>   Dante, *see* Alighieri, Dante
>   Empson, William:
>   >   *Argufying* 100
>   >   and I. A. Richards 102
>   >   *see also* Practical Criticism

To indicate a point in the text where a key distinction or contrast is drawn, use the abbreviation 'vs' (no full stop, roman type) for 'versus', discounting 'vs' in the alphabetical sequence. For example:

>   audience figures 63, 79-82
>   >   television vs cinema 65-67
>   *Heimatfilm*:
>   >   vs *Bergfilm* 95
>   >   plot structure 88, 90

Special features, such as pages with illustrations or with substantial bibliographical references, may be indicated by bold or italic numerals, but such devices should be used sparingly.

For inclusive numbers, use the convention specified in §5.2, e.g. '301–03' (not '301–3' or '301–303') but '1098–1101' (not '1098–101').

Page references to footnotes should be given in the form '41 n. 3', meaning note 3 on page 41. There should be spaces on either side of 'n.'. If two notes on the same page are referred to, use the form '41 nn. 3 & 4', with an ampersand.

Avoid 'ff.' where an explicit page range can be given: for instance, '34–37' rather than '34 ff.'. Similarly, avoid using 'f.' to mean 'and the page after'.

Index

abbreviations:
    edn for edition §7.3(a)
    for scientific units and other measures §5.5
    non-italicization of §3.7(b)
    shortened book titles §2.9
    use of full stop §2.10
    when to use §2.9
academic degrees §2.10
accents:
    in loan words §2.2
    on capital letters §3.6
access dates for websites §6.3
AD and CE §1.2(c), §5.1
ALA-LC §1.2(f)
albums:
    citing §7.8
alphabetical order §8.2
American states §2.10
American vs British spelling §2.1
angle brackets, *see* punctuation marks
apostrophe, *see* punctuation marks
arabic script §1.2(f)
Arabic, transliteration of §1.2(f)
art, works of:
    citing §1.3(b), §7.9
articles (a, an, the):
    casing in titles §3.4
    usage in alphabetical order §8.2
    usage in country names §4.1(b)
    usage in names of publishers §7.3(a)
articles (in journals):
    citing §7.4
author–date citation §7.1, §7.13

BC and BCE §1.2(c), §5.1, §5.2
Bible:
    capitalization §3.1
    citing from §7.3(d)
    non-italicization of §3.8(a)
bibliographies:
    accompanying author–date citation §8.4
    accompanying citation in notes §8.3
    name inversion in §8.1
books:
    citing §7.3(a)
brackets and braces, *see* punctuation marks
British Isles §4.1(d)
British vs American spelling §2.1

capital letters §1.2(c)
    see also small capitals
capital letters, accents on §3.6
capitalization:
    early modern §3.4
    of descriptions of regions §3.1
    of names of cultural or ethnic groups §3.1
    of names of events and organizations §3.1
    of names of movements and periods §3.3
    of names of newspapers §3.4
    of names of political factions §3.3
    of personal titles and positions §3.2
    of roman numerals §5.3
    of subtitles §3.4
    of titles of works §3.4
    title casing §3.4
captions for figures §1.3(b)
Celtic personal names §4.3(d)
centuries §5.1, §5.3
changes of personal name §8.1
chapters in books:
    citing §7.3(b)
circa and *c*. §5.1
citations:
    abbreviated §7.12
    author–date system of §7.13
    from the Bible §7.3(d)
    in notes vs author–date §7.1
    of chapters in edited books §7.3(b)
    of cover versions of songs §7.8
    of dictionary entries §7.5
    of entire books §7.3(a)

of exhibition catalogues §7.9
of films §7.8
of individual poems §7.3(b)
of interviews §7.11
of journal articles §7.4
of letters §7.11
of manuscripts §7.7
of newspaper articles §7.6
of plays and longer poems §7.3(c)
of recorded music §7.8
of software §7.8
of television programmes §7.8
of unpublished theses §7.10
of web pages and social media posts §7.5
of works of art §7.9
place and date of publication §7.3(a)
software for generating §1.2(h)
classical names §4.3(a)
colons, *see* punctuation marks
commas, *see* punctuation marks
composers §7.8
compound nouns:
   hyphenation of §3.5
conference papers:
   citing §7.10
copyright:
   acknowledging in figure captions §1.3(b)
   of letters and interviews §7.11
   poems and song lyrics §2.14
correspondence:
   citing §7.11
cover versions of songs:
   citing §7.8
cross-references:
   in indexes §8.7
   in main text §1.2(h)
   where an author or artist has more than one name §8.2
currency §5.4
Cyrillic script §1.2(f)
Cyrillic, transliteration of §1.2(f)

dashes, *see* punctuation marks
dates §5.1
   access dates for websites §6.3
definite article:
   discounted in alphabetical lists §8.2
   for country names §4.1(b)
   omitted from names of journals §7.4
   omitted from names of newspapers §7.6
   omitted from names of publishers §7.3(a)
degrees, academic §2.10
deutschmark §5.4
diacritics, *see* accents
dictionary entries:
   citing §7.5
dissertations:
   citing §7.10
DOIs:
   availability of §6.1
   format to follow §6.2
   in citations of books §7.3(a)
   in citations of journal articles §7.4
Dutch and Flemish personal names §4.3(d)

ebooks:
   citing §7.5
   lack of page numbering in §7.3(a)
Egyptian hieroglyphs §1.2(f)
em-rule, *see* punctuation marks
emojis §7.5
en-rule, *see* punctuation marks
endnotes:
   numbers §2.16(a)
   punctuation in §2.16(b)
England §4.1(d)
et al., deprecation of §7.3(a), §8.3
European currencies §5.4
exclamation mark, *see* punctuation marks
exhibition catalogues:
   citing §7.9

Facebook §7.5
facsimile reprints §7.2, §7.3(a)
figures §1.3(a)
film stills, captions for §1.3(b)
films:
   citing §7.8
fol. and fols §7.3(a), §7.7
font to use for text §1.2(b)

footnotes:
    numbers   §2.16(a)
    punctuation in   §2.16(b)
franc   §5.4
French personal names   §4.3(d)

general editor   §7.3(a)
graphemes   §1.2(g)
Great Britain   §4.1(d)
Greek script   §1.2(f)
guidelines for authors   §1.1

Han (Chinese, Japanese, or Korean)
    script   §1.2(f)
hard sign ъ   §1.2(f)
Harvard-style citation, see author-date citation
hashtags   §7.5
headings and subheadings   §1.2(d)
Hebrew script   §1.2(f)
hyphenation:
    of adjectives and adverbs   §2.6
    of compound nouns   §3.5
    of place names   §4.1(c)
hyphens, see punctuation marks

ibid.   §2.16(b)
illustrations, see figures
image files   §1.3(a)
in-text references, see author-date citation
indexing:
    cross-references   §8.7
    name inversion in   §8.1
    organization   §8.6
    sub-entries   §8.6
    what to index   §8.5
initials   §4.3(e)
International Phonetic Alphabet   §1.2(g)
Internet Movie Database   §6.3
interviews:
    citing   §7.11
    copyright on   §7.11
inverting names   §8.1
italicization:
    of abbreviated journal names   §2.10
    of foreign terms   §3.7(b)
    of loan words   §3.7(b)

of punctuation   §2.11
of titles of films and works of
    art   §3.8(b)
of titles of works   §3.8(a)
of words or terms under
    discussion   §3.7(a)
-ize vs -ise   §2.1

journals:
    abbreviated names of   §2.10
    availability of DOIs in   §6.1
    capitalization in names of   §3.4
    citing articles from   §7.4
    reprints from   §7.2
    special issues of   §7.4
justification of text   §1.2(a)

krone   §5.4

l. and ll.   §2.9, §2.16(b)
letter alphabetization   §8.2
letters:
    citing   §7.11
    copyright on   §7.11
loan words:
    accents in   §2.2
    italicization of   §3.7(b)
    plural spellings of   §2.4

manuscripts   §7.7
Microsoft Word   §1.1, §1.2(a), §1.2(h)

names:
    Celtic personal names   §4.3(d)
    Dutch and Flemish personal
        names   §4.3(d)
    French personal names   §4.3(d)
    historical place names   §4.1(a)
    inversion of   §8.1
    of academic institutions   §4.2
    of artists   §1.3(b)
    of authors and editors in
        citations   §7.3(a)
    of cities and countries   §4.1(b)
    of classical authors   §4.3(a)
    of kings and queens   §4.3(c), §8.1
    of movements   §3.3, §3.5

of popes and saints §4.3(b)
of publishers §7.3(a)
patronymics in §8.1
Russian personal names §4.3(d)
use or omission of middle names §8.1
newspapers:
   accessed online §6.3
   capitalization of names §3.4
   citing §7.6
note numbers §2.16(a)
number ranges §2.7, §5.2
numbering:
   of centuries §5.3
   of figures §1.3(a)
   of footnotes and endnotes §2.16(a)
   of tables §1.4
   roman numerals §5.3

Old Style dates §5.1
online resources, *see* DOIs; URLs
open-access material and repositories §7.10

p. and pp. §2.9, §2.16(b), §7.3(a)
page layout §1.2(a)
page numbering §1.2(a)
parentheses, *see* punctuation marks
patronymics §8.1
permalink §6.3
peseta §5.4
PhD vs Ph.D. §2.10
phonemic notation §1.2(g)
phonetic notation §1.2(g)
photographs:
   captions for §1.3(b)
   citing §7.9
place names:
   historical §4.1(a)
   hyphenation of §4.1(c)
plays:
   citing §7.3(c)
   quotations from §2.15
plurals §2.4
poems:
   citing §7.3(c)
possessives §2.3, §4.4
pseudonyms, in indexes and bibliographies §8.1
publication date and place §7.3(a)

publishing houses, formatting names of §7.3(a)
punctuation:
   brackets inside brackets §2.8
   of notes §2.16(b)
   quotations inside quotations §2.13, §7.3(b)
   when to italicize §2.11
   within quotations §2.12(c)
punctuation marks:
   2-em rule, in bibliographies §2.7, §8.3
   angle brackets, to delimit URLs §6.3
   apostrophe, marking possessives §2.3
   brackets, for parenthetical statements §2.8
   colon:
      to divide title and subtitle §7.3
      used in DOIs §6.2
   comma:
      omission where unnecessary §2.5(d)
      to apply a relative clause to a category §2.5(b)
      to delimit phrases §2.5(a)
      to divide lists §2.5(c)
   dollar sign, for currency §5.4
   double quotation marks, for quotations within quotations §2.13
   em-rule:
      as parenthesis §2.7
      doubled as ditto mark §2.7, §8.3
      to introduce dialogue §2.12(c)
   en-rule:
      for numerical spans §2.7
      use in compound words §2.7
   euro sign, for currency §5.4
   exclamation mark, in quotations §2.13
   full stop:
      at end of long quotation §2.14
      for initials in personal names §4.3(e)
      marking abbreviations §2.10
   hyphen, in place names §4.1(c)
   hyphens §2.6, §3.5
   non-English quotation marks §2.12(c)
   question mark, in quotations §2.13
   single quotation marks:
      to delimit quotations §2.13

to enclose translations §2.12
used in long quotations §2.14
slash:
    use in DOIs §6.2
    use in URLs §6.3
square brackets:
    for editorial additions §2.8
    to indicate omissions §2.12(d)
stroke, to mark line division in
    poetry §2.13
Yen sign, for currency §5.4

quotation marks, *see* punctuation marks
quotations §2.12
    from plays or scripts §2.15
    long §2.14
    omissions from §2.12(d)
    short §2.12(a), §2.13
    when to display §2.12(a)

ranges and spans §2.7, §5.2
referencing, *see* citations
repositories of manuscripts §7.7
repositories of open-access articles §7.10
reprints §7.2
roman numerals §5.3
Russian personal names §4.3(d)

Scandinavian letters in alphabetical
    order §8.2
scholarly editions §7.2
    online-only §7.3(a)
    still in progress §7.3(a)
    with author's name in title §7.3(a)
series (of books) §7.3(a)
sig. and sigs §7.3(a)
single quotation marks, *see* punctuation
    marks
small capitals:
    for books of the Bible §7.3(d)
    for postcodes and some
        abbreviations §1.2(c)
    for volume numbers of books §5.3
social media §7.5
soft sign ь §1.2(f)
software:
    citing §7.8
    for generating citations §1.2(h)

for indexing §8.5
songwriters §7.8
spacing:
    after French punctuation §1.2(e)
    avoiding multiple spaces §1.2(e)
    of lines §1.2(a)
special issue of a journal §7.4
spellings:
    British vs American §2.1
    early modern §2.12(b)
    hyphenated or not §2.6, §3.5
    -ize vs -ise §2.1
    names of canonical authors §8.1
    plurals §2.4
    words ending in é §2.2
square brackets, *see* punctuation marks
sub-headings §1.2(d)

tables of data §1.4
television programmes:
    citing §7.8
television stills, captions for §1.3(b)
theses:
    citing §7.10
titles:
    abbreviated §2.9
    alternative titles with 'or' §7.3(a)
    capitalization of §3.4
    containing other titles §2.11
    italicization of §3.8(a)
    of books in citations §7.3(a)
    of exhibitions §3.8(c)
translation:
    of quotations §2.8
    of titles of books and films §3.8(d)
transliteration:
    of Arabic §1.2(f)
    of Cyrillic §1.2(f)
    of Russian names §4.3(d)
Twitter/X §7.5

units for scientific measurements §5.5
URLs:
    changing nature of §6.1
    format to follow §6.3
    when citing websites and social
        media §7.5

volume numbers:
    for journals §7.4
    for multi-volume works §7.3(a)
    small capitals for §7.3(a)

Washington, DC §2.10
Wayback Machine §6.3
websites:
    citing §7.5

inclusion in bibliographies §8.3
individual pages within large §6.3
weights and measures §5.5
Welsh personal names §4.3(d)
Welsh place names §4.1(b)
word alphabetization §8.2
works cited, *see* bibliographies

www.ingramcontent.com/pod-product-compliance
Lightning Source LLC
Chambersburg PA
CBHW050033090426
42735CB00022B/3470